D1588077

SIR ADAM FERGUSSON
Third baronet of Kilkerran
From the portrait at Kilkerran by Sir Henry Raeburn

LOWLAND LAIRDS

LOWLAND LAIRDS

by

JAMES FERGUSSON

FABER AND FABER LIMITED
24 Russell Square
London

*First published in mcmxlix
by Faber and Faber Limited
24 Russell Square London W.C.1
Printed in Great Britain by
R. MacLehose and Company Limited
The University Press Glasgow*

PATRI DILECTO
DUCI, COMITI, EXEMPLARI

FOREWORD

Of the essays in this book, No. 1 appeared originally in the *S.M.T. Magazine* (now *Scotland's Magazine*), Nos. 2 and 3 in the *Scots Magazine*, and Nos. 7 and 8 in the *Cornhill Magazine*. All have been revised and expanded, No. 1 considerably so.

No. 9 was written as a biographical preface to Lord Hermand's *Consistorial Decisions*, published in 1940 by the Stair Society, and is here slightly shortened.

The remaining essays, Nos. 4, 5, and 6, written in 1947–48, now appear in print for the first time.

J. F.

CONTENTS

9

ILLUSTRATIONS

THE LANDED FAMILIES OF LOWLAND SCOTLAND

The popular view of history tends to regard it in terms of the biography of monarchs and nobles. Occasional critics of to-day prefer to treat it in terms of economics or of nationalism, as the movement of vast impersonal forces. But in Scotland there is an increasing tendency to speak and write of the history of the Scottish *people*, as though their comparatively modern integration had existed much earlier than extant records suggest. It would be no more misleading, and might even be a useful counter-balance, to write the story of our country as that of the landed families of Lowland Scotland. For their influence on Scotland's growth and development has been steadier and more enduring than that of kings and regents, and far more direct than that of popular movements.

There have indeed been moments when the destiny of the whole nation turned on that of a single one of these families. It was two Lowland houses, the Bruces and the Stewarts (first established in Annandale and Renfrewshire respectively), who intermarried with the ancient royal family and founded the line of kings which came in time to rule all Britain. After them more than one of the great Lowland families held at times the government of the kingdom, and occasionally even the person of the sovereign, in their strong, ambitious hands, treading the narrow path to power that lay, perilous but fascinating, between banishment and the block. Of the Highland clans which play so much more flamboyant and conspicuous a part in popular history and in fiction, there was only one—and that

13

more open than most of them to the contacts and influences of the Lowlands—that travelled that path: Clan Campbell, through a succession of outstanding chiefs, exercised for a time as much influence on the political fortunes of Scotland as had the Douglases, the Crichtons, the Hamiltons, the Maitlands, and the Boyds.

But it is not these families, glorious or notorious, in whose records we should really study the growth of Scotland. It is rather in those of the small lairds, the knights, the 'landit men', whose names crowd the local and national registers. Yet all the landed families, of whatever rank or extent, blend and join in a complicated tangle of relationships which unites them all. It is impossible to trace the genealogy of any long-established family of the Lowland gentry without finding that its blood includes strains from similar families scattered over the length and breadth of Scotland, as well as linking it with the nobility on the one hand and the merchants of the burghs on the other. Class distinctions were never strong in Scotland. Earls' families intermarried with knights', the small laird wedded the daughter of the great, and the great laird might choose his bride from the daughters of a prosperous burgess—while that burgess himself might be the son or grandson of some cadet of a noble house. A complicated web of marriages related the duke to an Edinburgh merchant, and the king himself to an Ayrshire knight. The proverb that 'every Stewart's no sib to the king' gained its point from the fact that a good many Stewarts were.

Thus these Lowland families were bound to each other by ties of kinship which, often renewed, were always remembered with affection and pride. The Lowland Scot is proverbial for his scrupulous tracing of remote ancestors of the past and almost equally remote cousins of the present—a trait which he derives from his Celtic and Norse forbears and shares with their modern descendants. This pride of kinship and of name bound Scott to Scott and Kennedy to Kennedy as surely as Campbell clove to Campbell and Fraser to Fraser.

But if it was kinship that bound these landed families

together, it was the land itself that bound them to the classes that were landless. Between the laird and his tenant and even his servant there remained a kinship of feeling, a realisation of common interest, a sense of loyalty to the soil on which and from which both of them lived, which in comparison scarcely existed between English squires and English yeomen, and never came to birth between the French *seigneur* and his serfs. It arose partly from the feudal relationship which bound 'the Laird's Jock' to the Laird as it bound Harden to Buccleuch and Buccleuch to the king; partly from a common simplicity of life and manners; and partly perhaps from a community of race, since the Norman strain was assimilated in the Scottish nobility instead of overlaying society with an alien aristocracy, as happened in England. This relationship was maintained after the Reformation by the educational system which, till well on in the nineteenth century, sent the sons of laird, farmer, smith and fisherman to sit side by side on the same school bench. Ramsay of Ochtertyre testifies that there was 'a kindness and familiarity between the gentry and their people which proved very propitious to the latter'.[1] The laird and his men fought together in battle, or went curling or salmon-spearing together in peace, in a spirit of comradeship and knowledge of each other which flourished as long as Scotland remained a predominantly agricultural country, and is far from dead even now.

Even the merchant or the lawyer whose business lay in the towns felt the pull of this freemasonry of the soil, and tried, when he had amassed his fortune, to return to the life he or his forbears had left. All through the eighteenth century can be traced the rise of this or that family from a founder who, himself often the son or grandson of a Fife, Lothian or Border laird, bought an estate within a day's journey of Edinburgh, and strove to learn the mysteries of agriculture with as much assiduity as he ever bestowed on Craig and Stair or on the reports of skippers from the Low Countries and the Carolinas.

[1] *Scotland and Scotsmen in the Eighteenth Century*, ed. Alexander Allardyce, 1888, vol. ii, p. 190.

Thus the land united those it nourished. Dandie Dinmont felt quite at home with Counsellor Pleydell, and Cuddie Headrigg sat, although below the salt, at the same table as the laird of Milnwood. A friendly independence and a man-to-man recognition of each other's qualities warmed the relations of the Laird with the Laird's Jock. Only in the Lowlands of Scotland could there exist that peculiar blend of loyalty and informality—and macabre humour—enshrined in the anecdote of the laird's man who was to be hanged. The unfortunate man was lingering in his cottage when the laird strolled down to watch the ceremony; the goodwife entertained the laird with light conversation for some minutes, but her man, not unnaturally, still hesitated to emerge and meet his fate. At last the woman turned and cried through the doorway, 'Come awa', Jamie—come awa' to your hangin', and dinna vex the laird!'[1]

The entwined strands of loyalty to the land and loyalty to the blood make up the history of the Lowland families. They clung to the land and the land clung to them. It was not only the great earldoms, like Crawford and Rothes and Erroll, that passed down through families whose origins were almost prehistoric. Families like Balfour of Balfour, Haig of Bemersyde, MacDowall of Garthland, Scrymgeour-Wedderburn of Wedderburn, and Swinton of Swinton have roots that lie far back beyond the Ragman Roll, and have remained as landmarks in the changing scene of Scotland, their fortunes rising and falling with their country's. Some, like the great house of Douglas, began in a little upland valley and spread till their branches and alliances covered whole shires. Others, like Buccleuch and Cassillis, grew and consolidated themselves in smaller, solider units till they became little tyrants in their own districts,

[1] I give this story as I know it by tradition. There is another version in the Rev. James Hall's *Travels in Scotland* (1807), p. 404, where it is attached to Ballindalloch on Speyside. Hall was not the last to fail to see the story's humour. It is quoted in all seriousness by, e.g., Mr Thomas Johnston in his *History of the Working Classes in Scotland* and Professor Wallace Notestein in his recent book *The Scot in History* as an illustration of feudal tyranny.

LANDSCAPE ILLUSTRATING WORK OF THE 'IMPROVERS'

Foreground, road (*late eighteenth century*); centre, left, home farm (*middle nineteenth century*); centre, fields bordering river cleared of woods, drained, and enclosed (*middle eighteenth century*); beyond, woods around mansion-house (*early eighteenth century*); above, modern plantations.

waging small wars of their own and lording it over neighbouring families equally old but less dynamic: it was not for nothing that the Earls of Cassillis were nicknamed 'the kings of Carrick' or that one Buchanan of Arnprior styled himself 'king of Kippen'.

When the central government was weak, it was not only the nobles who took advantage of its incapacity. There are frequent instances in official records, especially of the sixteenth and early seventeenth centuries, of shameful violence, rapacity and treachery on the part of some of the lairds, which all too often went unpunished. A few, like the Mures of Auchendrane, suffered for their crimes in the end. But many enjoyed careers of scandalous success, like Alexander Forrester of Garden, who died in his bed in 1598 after terrorising a large part of Stirlingshire for nearly thirty years in a manner which would have done credit to a Chicago gangster of the 1920's.

Many landed families, however, appear with credit in crisis after crisis of Scotland's history as though always on the watch for their country's need of them. Such were the Maules of Panmure, who traced their origin from France of the early eleventh century. A Maule fought at the Battle of the Standard in 1138; another died in an heroic defence of Brechin Castle against the troops of Edward I in 1303; a third fell at Harlaw in 1411, and a fourth at Flodden in 1513; a fifth fought at Pinkie in 1547, and was taken prisoner shortly afterwards with his father at Panmure by English troops from Broughty Castle; his grandson loyally supported King Charles I, who created him an earl; two of that earl's sons fought against Cromwell at Dunbar, and one of them at Worcester too; and the fourth and last earl fought under Mar at Sheriffmuir, forfeiting thereby his honours and estates.

This is a record to stir the heart; yet the deeds it commemorates leave nothing behind them but examples of loyalty and valour. The true services of the Lowland families to Scotland were less romantic but more enduring.

It was the smaller lairds, especially those of the west country from the Clyde to the Solway (the class and the province that produced William Wallace), who were strongly influential in two of the greatest changes in post-Renaissance Scotland, and may perhaps be reckoned chiefly responsible for them. First, it was they who built up the young Church of Scotland, swung over the mass of the rural population to the cause of the National Covenant, and headed that stubborn and aggressive resistance to the royal authority throughout the 'Killing Times' which is at once the glory and the shame of the later seventeenth century in Scotland. Secondly, it was they, a century later, who, beating their swords into plough-shares, turned Scottish agriculture from a clumsy medieval craft into a modern science. In this great reform, which founded the Scottish farmer's present reputation, it was the Lothian lairds who led the way. Others followed them, especially in Ayrshire, Angus and Aberdeenshire, with eager and far-seeing experiments, setting an example to the rest of the country. From this class came Grant of Monymusk, Maxwell of Arkland, Cockburn of Ormistoun, Dempster of Dunnichen, Barclay of Urie, Fullarton of Fullarton, Orr of Barrowfield, Lord Kames, Lord Gardenstone and—though he was not exactly a Lowlander, nor a Highlander either—Sir John Sinclair of Ulbster.

The 'improvers' did not stop at farming. Many of them started programmes of afforestation, the earliest in the time of Queen Anne, whose results transformed the countryside; and their public-spirited zeal was responsible for countless other features of the Scottish landscape to-day: roads, bridges, piers, schools and churches; besides a few complete villages which in our own day are winning tributes of admiration as early examples of 'planning', and several towns originally founded as 'burghs of barony'.

In the agricultural reforms that distinguished the eighteenth and early nineteenth centuries, there can often be traced a consistent and hereditary policy through the annals of a single family. I devote one chapter of this book to the example of which I have closest personal knowledge. But its record could no doubt be paralleled in many parts of Lowland Scotland.

Some of the achievements of the improving lairds demanded not only energy and foresight but the courage to risk experiments which might bring success or, in not a few cases, disaster. But the adventurous spirit of these families was not always confined to their own countryside. From them, during the reigns of the Stewart kings, came that steady stream of soldier-adventurers who made the European reputation of Scotland as a nursery of warriors. Scott drew this type of Lowland wanderer in Dugald Dalgetty and Ludovic Lesly. Besides these, there were the merchants who established themselves in the seaports of France, Scandinavia, the Baltic, and the Low Countries, and the students who found their way to Paris, Padua, Leyden or Cologne. Many of these wanderers were cadets of landed families in Lowland Scotland. From some sprang new families that flourished in alien soil and often rose to the highest distinction in courts, camps or municipalities. Such were the Craufurds in Sweden, the Barclays in Russia, the Hamiltons and Hepburns in France, the Balfours in the Netherlands, and the Keiths and Leslies in Germany. Europe welcomed and absorbed Scotland's great export of younger sons. A modern German historian has reckoned that 'some 2,500 Scottish families sought their fortunes in East Prussia, West Prussia, and Pomerania' between 1500 and 1700.[1]

By no means all were adventurers. Some went abroad in fulfilment of a tradition, like the officers of the Scots Brigade, which won glory as the senior regiment in the Dutch service for nearly three hundred years, and 'never lost a stand of colours'. 'All the officers', says its historian, were 'persons of those families whom the more numerous class of the people in Scotland have from time immemorial respected as their superiors.' Nearly all were Lowlanders: Erskines, Grahams, Hendersons, Halketts, Douglases, Fergusons, Hays, Hamiltons and Scotts, but above all Balfours.[2]

[1] *Scottish Historical Review*, vol. xxvii, p. 187.
[2] See *The Scots Brigade in the Service of the United Netherlands*, ed. James Ferguson (Scottish History Society), 1899, vol. i, pp. xxv–xxvi.

After the Union and with the growth of the British Empire, this export was diverted into other channels. The enthusiasm which had manned the Darien expeditions helped to fill the new colonies in North America—and ultimately to stiffen their resistance to the British Government. Politics, the law, the universities, and the church offered opportunities to others. Scotland had never been a rich country, and even through the eighteenth century economic pressure continued to drive able and ambitious younger sons to seek their fortunes in Edinburgh, in England, and overseas.

Many of the lairds, or their younger brothers, went into Parliament, and it was from established Lowland families that there came such men as George Baillie of Jerviswood, Sir Gilbert Elliot of Minto, James Oswald of Dunnikier, Sir William Pulteney (who was born a Johnstone of Westerhall but changed his name), Alexander Wedderburn, who became Lord Chancellor of England, George Dempster of Dunnichen, and above all Henry Dundas. Through the 'interest' wielded by every owner of an old estate, which might extend from the control of one or two votes or of a single burgh to the votes of half a county, the landed Lowland families, for more than a century after the Union of the Parliaments, in effect returned the majority of the Scottish members. These members generally displayed a high standard of ability, integrity and public spirit, in strong contrast to the English back-bencher of the same period. It must have been from them that Horace Walpole formed his opinion of the Scots as 'the most accomplished nation in Europe',[1] since they were at that time (1758) almost the only Scots he had ever met. The biographies of such men are conclusive evidence against the popular view that 'corruption' and a severely limited electorate produced in the eighteenth century an inferior type of legislator to that which followed the first Reform Bill. They brought to politics the same eager energy which their brothers gave to law, business, farming, philosophy or antiquarian researches, according to their bent.

[1] *The Works of Horatio Walpole, Earl of Orford* (*Catalogue of Royal and Noble Authors*), 1798, vol. i, p. 492.

At the turn of the century the foresight and influence of Henry Dundas provided a further outlet for his young country-men in the service of the East India Company. Thereafter the contribution of the Lowland Scots to the growth of British India, the Colonies, and later the Dominions becomes too vast for me to trace here. It has been very well and agreeably described by Professor A. Dewar Gibb in his book *Scottish Empire*.

A fairly large book might be made of the services rendered to Scotland, and to Britain, by Lowland families of a single name; for several have been notable for a special talent or apti-tude shown continuously for generation after generation. Examples are the Dalrymples and Dundases in law and politics, the Cochranes in scientific invention, and the Scotts and Elliots (since the time when war alone was 'the Borderers' game') in sheep-farming.

But all this great reservoir of energy and of talent was founded on the land, and the current of its force was impelled by the entwined sense of tradition and obligation which long association with the land and those who work on it inspires. This sense became, I think, more self-conscious and therefore more earnest in the Victorian Age, whose ideals of social duty were as marked in some spheres as they were absent in others. The Victorian outlook on life was very different from the Georgian, but in many ways the two periods are bound together, for the great age of the Lowland laird was from the Union of the Parliaments to the First World War. Throughout those two centuries the lairds were, by and large, secure on their hereditary estates, and continued steadily to breed large families, to bring them up in country ways, to instruct them in the traditions of public duty and of the responsibilities that go with hereditary privileges, and to send out a substantial proportion of them to the service of the country and, later, of the Empire.

But with the nineteenth century came the growth of large estates and the virtual disappearance of the small lairds. Some fell by the wayside in the race for agricultural reform, through 'improvements and speculations far beyond their capital, and often beyond the bounds of prudence,' as a writer of 1811 puts it. A hundred and forty Scottish landowners, nearly all west-country Lowlanders, were ruined by the failure of the Ayr Bank in 1772; many others suffered in the financial crisis that attended the outbreak of the French war in 1793. Many representatives of old houses, thus dispossessed, migrated to the cities or overseas. A few remained on the land as tenants instead of owners: there are farmers to-day with pedigrees much longer than their landlords'.[1] From the beginning of the nineteenth century, the large estates gradually absorbed the smaller properties, and the laird tended more and more to become a landowner only, with little or no interest in practical farming but leaving the cultivation of most of his estate to his tenants while bearing himself the responsibilities of fencing, draining, building, repairing and planting.

Yet there still lived on the tradition that the laird and his dependants shared a kinship with the soil rather than the impersonal relationship of employer and employed; and the position of tenants and of estate craftsmen often became almost as hereditary, in practice, as that of the laird himself. Indeed one old Ayrshire farming family, the Howies in Lochgoin, claim to have remained on the same farm as tenants for forty-two generations. Where this tradition was forgotten, to the hurt of all concerned, it was oftener by city-bred purchasers of estates than by the old-established families. There were instances, it is true, of harsh treatment of tenants, and also of reprehensible apathy regarding the living conditions of employees—though this last should be regarded in the light of the commonly accepted health standards of that time. But there were no clearances in the Lowlands like those that darken the history of a few of the large Highland estates. The best of the Lowland lairds carried on a patriarchal rule which went far beyond the

[1] Well within living memory there died an old Border farmer who was reputed to be by direct descent the last of the Blackadders of Blackadder. One ancestor of his fell at Flodden, and the family was old even then.

mere ownership of the land or the mere direction of a business. It took account of amenities as well as—often in preference to —profits, and included a personal interest in the welfare of every member of their employees' families. It built, in good solid stone and with an eye to both comfort and beauty, farmhouses and cottages that were homes for people and not, as in the miners' rows or the bleak impersonal streets of the new manufacturing towns, mere hutches for 'labour'. Cockburn of Ormistoun was not the only laird, nor the last, who could truly say, 'No father can have more satisfaction in the prosperity of his children than I in the welfare of those on my estate.'[1]

I write as a partisan—and why not? The bad lairds have had plenty of publicity, if not more than they deserved: the good not so much. They should be remembered not as picturesque antiques, but for what they did. They cared for the land, and for their dependents, with as much thought as does the modern State, and often with more discrimination. To them, too, Scotland owes all its finest woodlands, a quantity of noble architecture, and collections, great and small, of pictures, books, and furniture which have made the Scottish country mansion a living and harmonious example of our culture at its best.

Many such treasures, which once enriched the life of a family in its own home, and formed, in a sense, a part of its private annals, have now passed into public galleries, museums and libraries for the delight and instruction of a nation; but those which still remain in their original settings draw a special glamour from the record of the past which they enshrine and preserve. No family portrait is ever quite the same in an art gallery as when looking down on the room in which its subject once lived.

The First World War wounded this rural society severely. Many estates were reduced, broken up, or changed hands, and some of the new owners acquired their lands without the tradi-

[1] *Letters of John Cockburn of Ormistoun to his Gardener,* 1727– 1744, Scottish History Society, 1904, p. xxiv.

tions which in past times had not failed to pass with them even to distant heirs or to purchasers. The survivors of the old lairds settled down to cope with new conditions, smaller estate staffs, and steadily rising costs, not merely of improvements, but of maintenance. Their sons—fewer now, because families were smaller—turned in many cases to business and commercial careers, for the means were now often lacking that might have sent them into the fighting services or maintained them to study for the law or enter Parliament. The Laird's Jock often found, as he grew up, that employment was not available for him, as it had been for his father, in the woods, the gardens, or the joiner's shop, and went off to Glasgow or Canada; and his sister did the same, instead of going, as her mother had done, into service at 'the big house'.

Between the First World War and the Second, the whole economy of landownership changed. In the nineteenth century, up to 1880, the farm rents had provided a large and steady revenue which allowed fruitful expenditure on estate improvements—illustrated by the enormous number of farm houses and steadings all over Scotland which date from the middle or late Victorian period—and yet left a considerable private income to be expended on plantations, gardens, shrubberies, the preserving of game, and a fairly opulent style of living. The lavishness of Victorian hospitality stimulated the enlargement or rebuilding of the old houses on a scale which presupposed a perpetual supply of domestic servants and of the means to support them. But the introduction of income tax, then of death duties, and finally the steadily rising scale of both, first cut off the private income and then ate into the revenue that maintained the estate; and farm rents, which had fallen steeply after 1880 when the produce of American and Canadian farming began to compete with home agriculture, never rose again to the peak figures of the 'seventies. The Second World War brought further increases in income tax, and also a long overdue rise in the wages of agricultural workers, a class which, in the terms of the Act, included foresters; this necessitated proportionate increases in the wages of all estate workers. Finally came a substantial increase in the employers' share of workers' insurance. Thus the lament which John Galt, in 1825, put into the mouth of the impoverished laird of Auld-biggings, in *The Last of the Lairds*, took on a new significance—'What with the Government at the one end with the taxes, and the labourous folk at the other with their wages, the incomes of our 'stated gentry is just like a candle lighted at both ends.'

Those estates which had such resources as timber, or which were scientifically farmed, in whole or in part, by their owners, managed to keep their heads above water. But their number slowly diminished, and improvements could not be carried on at the same pace as formerly, nor keep up with advances in agricultural methods and in the general standard of living. The ravages in timber plantations caused by the drastic fellings of the First World War were not nearly repaired when the Second brought even larger demands, and by 1945 the cost of replanting had trebled since 1939, while since that date the prices at which timber could be sold had been 'frozen'. Despite the country's urgent need for more afforestation, the growers of timber are not encouraged by the State as realistically as are the growers of food; for the financial return which the timber-grower is allowed is not equated to his production costs.

Landowners as a class are widely regarded as an anachronism, and, although they still have a not unimportant part to play in rural society, are being tacitly encouraged to disappear. But the laird who is not a merely inactive landowner is not dying out, though he is changing. There are two classes of lairds to-day, the old and the new. The new laird is often the former tenant farmer who has bought his farm, and perhaps an adjacent one as well. He enjoys a new independence and security. He is also assuming the burdens of maintenance, repairs, fencing and draining, which his landlord formerly bore. Sometimes he is the incomer with money from the city who has bought land and settled down to farm it, perhaps, like some of the new lairds of the eighteenth century, answering some dimly felt call in his blood from a long-dead ancestor who left the country for the town a century or two ago.

The old lairds for whom there is some definite future, apart from a few who have turned their estates into private companies, are those who have reduced their properties to the size of a large farm which they can and do run themselves, or to a forestry unit. Between these and the class of tenant farmers turned into what used to be called 'cock lairds', it looks as if rural Scotland may revert to a state comparable to that of the period before the beginnings of the Agricultural Revolution, becoming once more a country of small lairds with only a few large proprietors; the Crown, as before, being the largest, and the companies, municipalities and co-operative societies taking the place of the great landowners of the Middle Ages. If that is so, a new class of landed families will arise in the Lowlands, and it will be interesting to see if it absorbs the traditions of the old one. As the sons and grandsons of the new lairds succeed to properties which become hereditary, they will come to learn the social duties and responsibilities that make the possession of land not so much an ownership as a trusteeship.

On the other hand, it may prove impossible for that sense of trusteeship to survive without the inherited memory of the conditions that bred it. The lairds, in addition to their work in agriculture and afforestation, once exercised a number of functions which belong nowadays to the State, local authorities or incorporated bodies. These functions included, at one time or another, the administration of local justice through the baron courts, the drawing up of voters' rolls through the Michaelmas Head Courts,[1] the development of rural industries, the building of churches, schools, and occasionally whole villages. The lairds were responsible, too, for the upkeep of the public roads: not till 1792 did the State begin to assume some responsibility for maintaining at least the main highways.

A great deal of our rural landscape is the monument to the old lairds' discharge of their public duties, the responsibility

[1] See Holden Furber: *Henry Dundas*, 1931, pp. 179–181.

for which has now passed to other hands. But the spirit that once vitalised that responsibility must not perish: it must be directed into other channels, into conscientious service of the land itself, and into the innumerable committees, from those of a County Council downwards, through which local government is carried on. It is in this sphere that the traditions of the old lairds must be kept alive and renewed.

To those traditions Scotland owes a great debt. By their fidelity to them, the Lowland lairds provided her for centuries with leaders and pioneers in every activity of the national life from war to farming. They maintained a rural patriarchy which, at its best, gave security and healthy employment to most of the country population. Their estates were social as well as economic units, whose breaking up is a matter for regret, since the tendency of present-day legislators is to suppress the small social unit, with all its individuality and lively companionship, for the sake of the large—to merge the village in the town, and the town in the 'conurbation'. Their standards of civilisation demanded the best work of the Adams, the Foulises, the Edinburgh silversmiths, Ramsay and Raeburn, besides the skill of countless nameless craftsmen whose products are still an inspiration to the standards of to-day. Their ideals of public service contributed innumerable leaders to local administration, development and culture, whose names are unknown to history, and also such diversely eminent national figures as Dundas, McAdam, Abercromby, Cockburn, the Napiers, Balfour, Haldane, Cunninghame Graham, Haig, and Sir Herbert Maxwell.

The personalities studied in this book are of earlier periods than most of those just named. They were not chosen to prove any thesis advanced in the foregoing pages, but as types of human character whose activities light up some little known corners of Scottish history. There are good and bad among them, energetic and tranquil, single-minded and versatile; but each essay will, I hope, in its way illustrate something of what the Lowland lairds have contributed to the rich and fascinating fabric of Scottish life.

2

THE FORESTERS OF THE TORWOOD

One of the most picturesque titles among the minor officials of the old Scottish court was that of Hereditary Forester and Keeper of the Torwood. In the Torwood itself to-day only a few trees remain of what was once a large royal forest. Wallace and his men lurked in its glades, and many armies passed by it or through it during the troubled years of the Stewarts. Kings hunted there, and it was a royal preserve of timber. The Keepership of the Torwood was therefore a not unimportant post.

Like other and more eminent offices, the keepership became hereditary; and, as with those of steward, doorward or constable, the designation became a surname. By the reign of James II, if not earlier, there was an established family named Forrester of Torwood, and more than once in charters and records of the sixteenth century the Forresters are stated to have held their office 'beyond the memory of man'. Their duties included the prevention of timber-felling in the forest by unauthorised persons, and the maintenance of the dykes round its march which were supposed to keep deer inside it and cattle outside. In payment, the Keeper was allowed the right of 'bark and beuch', which a charter of 1609 defines as 'fallin wode with the bark and beuche of all treis that sall happin to fall or be cuttit within the said wode'.[1] His emoluments included a chalder of bear (a kind of barley) from 'the lordschip of Strivilingschire', which is described as 'his ordiner fee' and was paid to him yearly.[2]

[1] *Reg. Mag. Sig.*, vii, 58.   [2] *Exchequer Rolls*, xxiii, p. 8.

THE FORESTERS OF THE TORWOOD

The earliest of the family of whom I find record was Robert Forrester of Torwood, who died before 1464 and was succeeded first by one son, Alexander, and then by another, Malcolm. In James III's reign the lands of Torwood and Torwoodhead, with the office of forester and keeper of the Torwood, were held by Henry Forrester, Malcolm's son; but he and his father apparently had the bad luck or bad judgment to be on the wrong side at Sauchieburn. On 26 November 1488 the newly crowned King James IV granted the lands and office to 'Duncan Forestare de Gunnarschaw', who seems to have been a nephew of Malcolm Forrester.[1]

Duncan rose in the world rapidly. In 1480 he had been keeper of Stirling Castle, when payments were made to him for oatmeal for the watch-men and porter; and he was provost of Stirling almost continuously from 1477 to 1490. He is described in an old genealogy of the Buchanans[2] as 'a very toping[3] gentleman,' and it is clear that he rose rapidly in the favour of the King. On 17 September 1489 James 'hufe Duncan Forrester's sonnis barne,' in other words stood sponsor at his grandchild's baptism. By 1492 he was knighted, and on 31 July of that year the King appointed him Comptroller of his Household. A year later, 'as a special favour, and for his faithful service,' he was given the lands of Skipinch in Knapdale, 'with the castle, fortalice, and place of the same, extending to 4 merklands . . . united and incorporated into one free barony of Skipinch, with a reddendo of one silver penny.' Finally, early in 1496, the King granted 'to his servant and Comptroller Sir Duncan Forrester of Skipinch and to his heirs the lands of Garden-Sinclare, the tower and fortalice of the same, in the stewartry of Menteith and county of Perth,' with some other lands in Stirlingshire. Thus the Forresters were established as Forresters of Garden

[1] John C. Gibson: *Lands and Lairds of Larbert and Dunipace Parishes*, 1908, p. 134, note.

[2] *Ibid.*, p. 135.

[3] 'Topping—Fine; noble; gallant. A low word.'—*Johnson's Dictionary*, 1755.

(sometimes spelt Carden), and endured under that name for more than a hundred years. Other Forresters who flourished in Kintyre may have been their kinsfolk.[1]

In that same year Sir Duncan inscribed his name—'Duncan Forrester, kt.'—in a magnificent antiphonary or choral missal, a huge leather-bound volume with bronze clasps, which is now preserved in the church of the Holy Rude at Stirling.

Sir Duncan Forrester was for a period Comptroller of Queen Margaret's household, but returned to the charge of the King's in 1509. He seems to have enjoyed considerable favour with James. In November, 1508, there is a glimpse of their intimacy when it is recorded that the King played 'at the cartis with Schir Duncane Forestar and the Erle of Mountros', and the following evening 'playit at the tables with Schir Duncane Forestar' and apparently lost to him 'x Franch crounis'.[2] What sort of game was played 'at the tables' I cannot say, but the phrase recalls one of my favourite lines in *Antony and Cleopatra*:

Let it alone: come, let's to billiards.

In any case, these entries set Sir Duncan clearly among the figures of that bright court whose expenses he supervised and for whom he provided fire and plenishing, comforts and luxuries, the wax lights that shone in the halls of Stirling and Linlithgow, and

> *the new fresh wine*
> *That grew upon the river of Rhine,*
> *Fresh fragrant clarets out of France,*
> *Of Angers and of Orliance,*
> *With mony ane course of great daintie.*[3]

If he had only been a suitable butt for Dunbar's biting pen, like other members of the royal household, James Doig or Sir John Sinclair, he might have been assured of his little share of immortality.

Sir Duncan was twice married, first to Margaret Forsyth,

[1] See Andrew McKerral: *Kintyre in the 17th Century*, 1948, p. 93.
[2] *Treasurer's Accounts*, iv, 85.   [3] *The Dregy of Dunbar.*

the daughter of a laird in Clydesdale, by whom he had five sons and a daughter, and secondly, before 1503, to Margaret Bothwell, who bore him four sons and three daughters. His eldest son, Sir Walter Forrester, was given the office of forester and keeper of the Torwood in 1497, Sir Duncan being perhaps too much occupied with his duties at court to attend to the forest as well; and in 1508 he was also given the lands of Garden itself, the liferent being reserved to his father. The reddendo of Garden at this time is stated to be 'one red rose at the Feast of the Nativity of Saint John Baptist'—the anniversary of Bannockburn.

Sir Duncan seems to have died in 1526 or 1527, and his elder son Sir Walter within a few years after him. The latter was twice married and had several children. By his first wife, Agnes Graham, a sister of the Earl of Montrose who once played 'at the cartis' with his father and the King, Sir Walter was the father of Sir James Forrester of Garden, who also did not survive long. Sir James was provost of Stirling, 1528–30. He was married to Agnes Cockburn, widow of William Murray of Touchadam and mother of John Murray of Touchadam. Two of his rare appearances in contemporary records show him witnessing the two marriage contracts of his stepson: the first, which was not fulfilled, in 1518 to Catherine, daughter of John, fifth Lord Erskine; the second, which was, more than fourteen years later, to her younger sister Janet.[1]

To Sir James there succeeded, as laird of Garden and keeper of the Torwood, his son David, who was provost of Stirling in 1547 when he fell, like so many other lairds and noblemen, at the battle of Pinkie. He married Elizabeth Sandilands, daughter of James Sandilands of St. Monans, and left five sons. Another David Forrester was Keeper of the Torwood during the Regency of Marie of Lorraine, but the heir who ultimately succeeded to the hereditary office was Sir James's grandson Alexander, whose life is recorded in more detail than that of any other of his family.

[1] Historical Manuscripts Commission: *MSS of the Earl of Mar and Kellie*, pp. 8, 9.

It was not till 15 July 1575 that Alexander is recorded as having sasine of Garden, 'with the tower, fortalice, manor, and mill of the same'; but he appears as Alexander Forrester of Garden as one of the witnesses to the inventory, dated 20 March 1566–7, of the 'artailyearis and munitionis with plenissing' in Edinburgh Castle, made by Sir James Balfour of Pittendreich for Queen Mary, and he acted on this occasion as a representative of the Earl of Mar.[1] He was probably born about 1540 or a little earlier, being described in 1557 as 'an honourable young man' (*honorabilis adolescentulus*).

Alexander was a notable, indeed a notorious character in the Scotland of James VI. He has never been the subject of a biography, but his name appears very often in the records of the Privy Council, and nearly always as that of the protagonist in some scandalous misdemeanour or riot. He was not, however, by any means uncharacteristic of his generation. King James VI's vaunted peace through the pen seems to have been little if at all superior to that which his ancestors had maintained by the sword. But Alexander's behaviour is distinguished above that of other contemporary rascals by a certain braggadocio which makes his turbulent career well worth disentangling from the official records of his time.

He started life respectably, at any rate. In the early summer of 1557 he went to France with twelve companions, supported by a letter from the Queen Regent, Mary of Lorraine, to Queen Mary of England, requesting safe conduct for him through the latter's kingdom to France 'for his lefull [lawful] erandis and besinessis thair to be done'. Perhaps this was an early instance of the Grand Tour, since Alexander's object was merely to visit 'the partis in France and utherris beyound sey'.[2] By 1564 Alexander had the responsible post of 'keeper of the Queen's marts'. He was provost of Stirling, as were so many of his family at various times, in 1562–3, 1564–5, and in 1569–70. In 1569 he and his brother Robert (one of the bailies of Stirling) were two of the three commissioners representing that ancient

[1] *Op. cit., Supplementary Report*, p. 26.
[2] *Calendar of Scottish Papers*, xi, p. 197.

A VERY OLD OAK, ONE OF THE FEW TREES REMAINING OF THE ANCIENT TORWOOD

burgh at the Convention of Estates held in Perth, and at that upon the Regency after the Earl of Moray's assassination.

All this suggests the beginnings of a respectable career in the public service. In 1575 Alexander had sasine of Garden, and in 1588 King James VI granted to him, his eldest son James, and their heirs male whomsoever, the lands of Torhead, Torwood, and Torwoodhead, and the family dignity of 'heretabill forestar and kepar of the Torwod'.

Alexander had married, about 1568, Jean Erskine daughter of John Erskine of Dun, and had a quiverful of children, six sons and six daughters. One of the latter, Barbara, married David Livingstone, younger of Dunipace. Another, Christian, married Simon Fergusson, younger of Kilkerran, in Ayrshire, who died in 1591, leaving her with two young children; she later married Gilbert Ross, a notary to whom John, fifth Earl of Cassillis, gave the provostship of the Collegiate Church of Maybole in 1602.[1]

But quiet family life was anything but the ideal of Alexander Forrester. His crown office notwithstanding, he was one of the most audaciously unruly people in Stirlingshire, frequently at odds with his neighbours and with no respect whatever for the authority of his royal master. He was characteristic of the 'troublous time' which old Sir Richard Maitland of Lethington so constantly lamented:

> *Mair mischievous and wicked warld*
> *Nor there is now,*
> *Saw nane, I trow.*

The first evidence of Alexander's unneighbourly activity appears as early as 1573, when Sir William Douglas of Lochleven, the man who five years before had failed to keep Queen Mary a prisoner in his island castle, became surety in the sum of one thousand pounds that one Archibald Aitkin, dwelling in Alloa, should be 'harmeles and skaythles of the said Alex-

[1] See *Historie of the Kennedyis*, ed. by Robert Pitcairn, 1830, pp. 55-6.

ander'. Forrester had evidently been threatening Aitkin, and —to judge by the large security demanded—with considerable violence.

Alexander's next quarrel was with Thomas Bruce of Larber-scheles, and it illustrates with startling vividness his attitude towards his duties as keeper of the Torwood. Bruce held lands which marched with the Torwood, and owned cattle which showed a disposition to stray into the forest. This inconvenience should have been prevented by the dykes which Alexander was supposed to maintain, but he, having some grudge against Bruce, made a point of 'wilfully downehalding' them. As a result, Bruce was forced to pay a special cowherd to keep his cattle out of the forest. Sometimes, however, in wintertime, the cattle could not be prevented from making for the trees in search of shelter from the sharp winds blowing down from the Ochils; and when this happened Alexander and his servants amused themselves by wounding the wretched beasts —they 'schot and hochit' them, Bruce complained, 'to his gret skaith and heavie dampnage'. Possibly the aggressors had been inspired by a rather similar performance by the Earl of Lennox and his adherents a few years before in the neighbouring forest of Cumbernauld against the brother of Lord Fleming, of which the contemporary record says, 'They have slane and distroyed the deer of his forrest of Cummernauld, and the quhit ky and bullis of the said forrest, to the gryt destructione of polecie and hinder of the commonweill. For that kynd of ky and bullis . . . was not mantenit in ony uther partis of the ile of Albion, as is weill knawin.'[1]

The Privy Council summoned Alexander and ordered him to 'big and hald up ane sufficient dyke'. Also, knowing his ways by this time, they enjoined him to 'use gude neichtbour-heid to the said Thomas', and backed this up by commanding him to find caution in two hundred merks within twenty-four hours not to harm Thomas Bruce or his family, on

[1] *A Brief Note of the Thingis Done be the Erle of Lennox and his Adherentis* (supplement to Richard Bannatyne's Journal, ed. by John Graham Dalyell, 1806, p. 521).

pain of being declared a rebel.[1] Presumably this relieved Bruce of his 'gret skaith and heavie dampnage'; but bad blood remained between the Bruces and the Forresters, as will be seen.

The next victim of Alexander Forrester's temper was one of the ushers of the King's chamber, John Drummond of Slipper-field—the father of a baby son who was later to become famous as William Drummond of Hawthornden. It was on 15 July 1587 that caution was required for the safety of John Drummond, and on this occasion the now familiar procedure has enlarged itself: the cautioner is Sir James Stirling of Keir, the security is no less than two thousand pounds, and the aggressors are not only Alexander Forrester but his brothers Robert and John and several others of the name of Forrester. Two years later there is yet another complaint, this time from William, Commendator of Pittenweem, and Alexander seems not only to have extended his business of troubling his fellow-citizens as far as Fife, but to have begun bringing up his children to take a hand in it; for William's persecutors include not only Alexander's brothers Robert and John but his sons James and John as well. In the next dispute, which occurred in the summer of 1592, yet a third son, another Alexander, has been enrolled in the gang.

The injured party of 1592 was the same John Drummond of Slipperfield; and in the following year the Forresters were after him again. The episode of 1593 must be reckoned Alexander's masterpiece in the art of making himself a nuisance, since this time he apparently worsted the Privy Council itself. The cause of the trouble was a quarrel over the march between the estate of Torwood, of which Drummond had a tack, and the lands of Torhead, Kingsidemuir, and 'Forrester's Mansion', which were held in life-rent by the laird of Garden. The Forresters had apparently set out to terrorise their neighbour. It was 'notour to the haill cuntrey' that 'the Laird of Garden and his freindis . . . accumpanyit with a grite nowmer of armeit per-sonis, bodin in feir of weir'—the regular legal phrase for going

---

[1] *Privy Council Register*, iii, pp. 602-3.

about fully armed in what was nominally peace-time—had harried the unfortunate Drummond and 'persewit him for his bodilie harme and slauchter'.

Drummond made his complaint to the Privy Council, and they deputed three of their number, 'the Lordis of Quhitting-hame, Drumcairny, and Halyruidhouse', to visit the debatable ground and decide the dispute on the spot. This did not suit Alexander's book at all: presumably he knew that his case was weak. He accordingly made special preparations to receive the committee, with results that showed either that he had the whole countryside completely under his thumb or else that he enjoyed more popularity and support among his neighbours than might have been supposed. Whatever the means of per-suasion he employed, their effect was startling. When the Lords of the Council arrived at the Torwood on the appointed day, 24 September, they found Alexander awaiting them with a small army, no less than 'ane thowsand men on horse and fute, bodin in feir of weir'. The Lords did their best to carry out their mission with dignity. Alexander was desired to dis-miss his forces and to 'cum on the ground of the said landis with ten and himself, in sobir maner'. This he declined to do, and the discomfited Lords saw nothing for it but to retire to a neighbouring house and wait for two days in the hope that Alexander would come to his senses. On the 26th they started out for the Torwood again. But on the way two gentlemen of the neighbourhood warned them that if they took Drummond with them to the disputed march, 'thair wald nocht faill to be slauchter', since Alexander's private army had not been dis-banded. Indeed 'the said Laird, his sone [James] and freindis, with their haill forceis, wer of new gadderit, of evill mynd, altogidder inclynnit to blude'. As it would have been quite impossible to decide the case with any pretence to impartiality while one party was afraid to appear and the other was backed by a thousand armed men, there was nothing for the Privy Council's committee to do but return to Edinburgh.[1]

1595 was another lively year for the laird of Garden. One

[1] *P.C.R.*, v, pp. 98–100.

of the Forresters, either a son or a close relation of his, quarrelled with one of the Bruces of Airth, for the sufficient reason that they 'hapnit bayth to love ae woman'. Their friends on both sides took up the quarrel, and on 10 April Garden's sons 'invadit' or assaulted Bruce while he was in the company of Livingstone of Dunipace. A free fight ensued, rather as in the opening scene of *Romeo and Juliet*: there 'came more and more, and fought on part and part'. A friend of Dunipace's was wounded, and three or four would-be peacemakers, citizens of Stirling, were hurt in separating the combatants.

This little disturbance had a serious sequel. The enmity between the Forresters and the Bruces deepened into a formidable feud, and the Livingstones, notwithstanding the ties of blood between them and the Forresters, sided with the Bruces. Letters of the period reflect the anxiety with which peaceable men watched the growing fire. 'This late displesour fallin out betwix Dunipas and Garden is lyik to work much ill amang us,' wrote John Colville, an official of King James's court, on April 25th; and a week later it was reported that a coolness had arisen between Dunipace and the Earl of Mar, to whom, as hereditary Keeper of Stirling Castle, all the Forresters adhered. During May everything seemed to be quiet, but Colville was still nervous about 'private bruits'.

The explosion came on June 24th. John Livingstone, younger of Dunipace, and John Bruce, younger of Airth, with 'the clannit men of Levingstoun and Bruce', waylaid and murdered a bailie of Stirling named David Forrester near Kirkliston, as he was riding home from Edinburgh. He may have been Garden's brother. In any case, he was a trusted follower of the Earl of Mar, and the comment in a letter written the following day—'This will make a stirre, I thinck'— foreshadowed the fury with which Mar took up the matter in the highest quarter and demanded justice on the murderers of 'Davy Forrester'.

Various people wrote to Mar to clear themselves of complicity in the crime. One was Dunipace. Another was Lord

Livingstone, who declared, without specifically referring to the murder, 'I wes nevir upoun ony consultationis or devyses to harme your lordschip in honour, persoun, or freindis.' The Master of Elphinstone admitted having slain a servant of Mar's but offered compensation for the dead man's wife and children, and protested, 'Being sa laitlie cum of your lord-schipis hous, I am sorie frome my hairt that your lordschip, upoun ony consavit suspicioun of my privitie or allowance of David Forestare's slauchter, sould appeir to bear to me ony malice or evill will.' As for King James, he promised his support if Mar would pursue the criminals by legal methods. 'So', commented Colville naïvely on 28 June, 'I think Mar will first use form of law and then his power.'

The Earl did his best to provoke the Bruces and Living-stones to further violence so that he might be justified in using physical force against them, though he intended to take the King's hint and 'keep o' the windy side of the law'. He arranged for the dead man an impressive funeral procession from Edinburgh to Stirling on 12 July, and led it ostentatiously through the Bruce and Livingstone lands. The solemn *cortège* included a banner carried between two spears showing 'the picture of the defunct on a fayre cammess [canvas], payntit with the number of the shots and wounds, to appeare the mair horrible and rewthfull to the behalders'. With this pageant rode 'my lord in his jack' and six hundred of his supporters, presumably including Garden and his sons, 'with displayit baner, in feir of weir'. 'This forme is rare', wrote a contem-porary chronicler, 'and was never usit in Scotland before.' The funeral, however, passed off without incident if not without comment.

The Forrester murder case became a matter of high politics, involving the King, the Queen, the Chancellor, the Master of Glamis, and many other notable people. On 20 October, at Linlithgow, the King signed a warrant for the arrest of five men for the murder, none of whom had been among the princi-pals and all of whom had already removed themselves out of reach. Three of them were Livingstones, one was a servant of

Airth's, and the other was Patrick Bruce, son of Alexander Forrester's old opponent Thomas Bruce of Larberscheles. But Mar's vengeance was not satisfied. At length a diet was fixed for 20 December, when the parties in the case were to come to the Tolbooth of Edinburgh, 'for underlying the laws for the slaughter of the said David'. Soon afterwards the rumour reached Edinburgh that the Earl of Mar and Forrester of Garden on the one hand, and the sons of Airth and Dunipace on the other, had arranged for as many as possible of their friends to come to Edinburgh with them. Not unnaturally the authorities feared lest the state of virtual war existing in Stirlingshire might be brought into the very streets of the capital, 'to the break of his Hieness peace', as they expressed it with unconscious irony, 'and troubling of the gude and quiet estait of the country, beside the hindering of justice'. To avoid another 'Cleanse the Causeway', they issued orders that none of the partisans of either side who was not concerned in the case was to approach Edinburgh, but should stay at home, 'unattempting onything quhilkis may ather hinder justice or move trouble or inconvenient . . . under the pane of deid without favour'. This prohibition having been imposed, the case was considered without further disturbance.[1]

In the course of the general clean-up of Stirlingshire which the authorities now attempted, Garden and his chief adherents were put to the horn. But they were not the men to submit to such a sentence without protest. They probably considered it grossly unjust.

On 30 December a pursuivant named John Roishill came to the Cross of Stirling to read the letters of horning publicly according to law. The Foresters had made their preparations to show what they thought of this ceremony. While Roishill was reading the document at the Cross, a band of the Foresters, headed by 'Garden's childring' John and Alexander, appeared before him armed with dags, pistollets, and other

---

[1] *Historie of King James the Sext*, pp. 346–7; *Calendar of Scottish Papers*, xi; *Letters of John Colville*; H.M.C., *MSS of the Earl of Mar and Kellie*, pp. 41, 45; *P.C.R.*, v, pp. 242–3.

weapons—in fact 'bodin in feir of weir' according to their habit. The wretched pursuivant was brutally assaulted. They 'pullit him doun of the said Croce, dang him with pistollettis on the heid, and, with the gairdis of their swerdis, cruellie hurte and woundit him in divers pairtis of his body, to the effusione of his blude in grit quantitie'; after which they 'violentlie and perforce' took his papers and tore them up. The Forresters refrained from actually killing the pursuivant, but this forbearance was lost on King James, who regarded such treatment of a royal emissary as a serious affront to his authority. 'His Majestie', wrote Colville on 7 January 1596, 'is much moved aganis the actoris, and thinkis Mar offendit in nocht apprehending thame.'[1]

On 28 January 1596 Garden and his sons were denounced as rebels. But Alexander himself, who was by now an old man, seems to have felt that his 'childring' had gone too far, and to have desired to end his days in peace if not in family unity. On 15 April King James signed in Stirling Castle a warrant registering a bond of assurance granted at his Majesty's desire by the Earl of Mar and Alexander Forrester of Garden to Alexander, Lord Livingstone, and Sir Alexander Bruce of Airth and their kin and friends. It declared that Garden was not to be responsible for the actions of a number of other Forresters—of Corstorphine, Strathhenrie, Logie, Culmoir, and Kipmad—who presumably still kept up the feud.[2] Less than two years later, on 13 January 1598, Alexander Forrester breathed his last. It was not till after his death that his sons received the royal pardon. On 11 April 1598 his eldest son and heir, Sir James Forrester, now of Garden, who had not taken part in the outrage at the Cross of Stirling, became surety for his brothers and their accomplices in a sum of £300 each, binding them to stay at Garden, which at that time lay within the borders of Perthshire, and not to enter the shires of Stirling and Linlithgow. With Alexander dead and his sons restrained, Stirlingshire must have seemed quite a peaceful place.

[1] *P.C.R.*, v, p. 261; Letters of John Colville, p. 190.
[2] H.M.C., *MSS of the Earl of Mar and Kellie*, pp. 45–6.

Alexander was buried in the Garden Chapel of the West Kirk of Stirling (now the Church of the Holy Rude), where the tomb of himself and his wife is still to be seen. It bears the arms of the Forrester and Erskine families, and the inscription round its edge commemorates Alexander Forrester on the reticent principle of *De mortuis nil nisi bonum*:

'Heir lyis ane honorabil mane calit Alexander Foster laerd of Garden quha deit the 13 of Januare 1598.'

The family never rose after his death to quite the same heights of notoriety. Sir James Forrester got into the comparatively prosaic trouble of debt. On 3 May 1609 Robert Nairn, advocate, had a charter from Sir James of the barony of Garden itself, on which he had lent its owner no less a sum than £3,000; 'but he was one of many creditors.'[1] Bit by bit Sir James had to part with most of the family property. Some of it, together with the office of forester and keeper of the Torwood, passed to the husband of his daughter Margaret—Sir William Ross of Muriestoun. Torhead, with the forest of the Torwood, he resigned in 1635 to George Forrester, head of the Forresters of Corstorphine, who had been created Lord Forrester by King Charles I when he visited Scotland two years before for his coronation.[2] These lands, as the free barony of Torwoodhead, remained in the possession of the Lords Forrester till the middle of the eighteenth century.

Stirling of Keir had acquired Garden from Robert Nairn within a year or two of Sir James Forrester's parting with it; he gave it to his second son, and from that owner descend the Stirlings of Garden who have possessed the property to the present day.

Sir James's early life had been more auspicious. In 1588 he married Margaret, daughter of John, fifth Lord Fleming, and in 1594 was present at Prince Henry's baptism at Stirling and received the honour of knighthood from King James after it. But after his father's death he too found himself at variance with authority. There was an action against him in 1609, when it appears that he had felled without permission the

---

[1] *Scots Peerage*, vol. vi, p. 392.   [2] *Ibid.*, vol. iv, p. 91.

best trees in the Torwood—no doubt in a desperate attempt to pay his debts by selling the timber. Again in 1617 he was in trouble for the same offence, when his indictment relates that 'the forest was well planted with timber, but it is now so defaced in sindrie parcellis and pairtis that there is not a tree to be seen'. What really seemed to pain the King's Advocate when making the charge was the tactless moment that Sir James had chosen to make free with the royal trees. For it was at this time that King James was paying the only visit he ever made to Scotland after he had forsaken the alarms of Edinburgh and Stirling for the peaceful ease of Whitehall—'now,' complained the Advocate, 'in this tyme of his Majesteis being in the cuntrey, and in the sicht of strangearis'![1]

In 1622 Sir James Forrester was ordered to the Tolbooth of Edinburgh for making an assault, with the assistance of a few friends, on a messenger-at-arms who was poinding some of his cattle. In the old Forrester manner, 'with many horribill aithes', they 'strak and dang the said compleiner with Jedburgh stalffis, and brak the same in peeceis on his persone.'[2] Seven years later Sir James was in worse trouble. He had been sent from the Edinburgh Tolbooth to Stirling Castle, where he petitioned for relief, being infirm in body. In the same year the little land he had left suffered in the sliding of a moss which, 'lyke ane thunder clap,' overflowed a number of small estates, making twenty families homeless and leaving 'nothing but the miserable face of a black mosse to looke unto in place of thair pleasant and fertile ground'.[3] In the gloom of these calamities the record of Sir James Forrester fades from sight.

Subsequent Foresters were comparatively law-abiding, and old Alexander Forrester would surely have despised an eighteenth century namesake of his, descended from the Garden family, who added to his coat-of-arms the craven motto, 'It's good to be lown'.[4] But another of our Alexander's children

[1] *P.C.R.*, xi, pp. 223–4.   [2] *Ibid.*, xii, pp. 719–20.
[3] Gibson, *op. cit.*, p. 147; *P.C.R.*, iv (second series), pp. 25–7.
[4] Alexander Nisbet: *A System of Heraldry*, 1722, p. 433. 'Lown' means 'calm'.

seems to have run more true to the family type. This was his daughter Christian, who lived to be an elderly woman in Ayrshire. Two months before her brother Sir James's second indictment for illegal tree-felling in the Torwood, there is recorded a complaint by one Alexander Barclay, 'merchant burgess of Edinburgh, now indweller in Mayboill', that he was going in fear of his life on account of Christian and her elder son by her first marriage, John Fergusson of Kilkerran. Barclay's story was that these two had caused him to be beset one Sunday morning as he was riding from Straiton to the parish church of Maybole; that he was attacked 'at the parting of the highway at Kirkmichael' by one of their kinsmen (a brother of George Fergusson of Threave) who bore the engaging nickname of 'Davie the Devill', with several accomplices, and that he had escaped only at the cost of a sword-cut in his neck, received through the double collar of his cloak.

Kilkerran and his mother denied the charges against them on oath, and were assoilzied. Davie the Devill was found guilty of the attack. He was unable to produce any evidence in support of his counter-charge that Barclay had attacked him first while he himself was on his way to church at Kirkmichael, and had put a pistol-bullet through his hat—'hard by his heid'.[1]

Part of Barclay's complaint was that for the last eight months Fergusson of Kilkerran and Davie the Devill had openly carried hackbuts and pistollets, contrary to the law. It is true that Ayrshire in those days—only a few years after the bloody feud between the Kennedys of Cassillis and of Bargany—was not much more tranquil than Stirlingshire. But one cannot help feeling that it may have been as much the Forrester blood transmitted through his turbulent mother as her actual instigation that bred in young Kilkerran his fondness for riding the roads of Carrick in the customary manner of the Forresters—'bodin in feir of weir'.

---

[1] *P.C.R.*, xi, pp. 234–5.

3

SOLDIER AND SPORTSMAN:
THOMAS MAULE OF PANMURE

Accident is often the cause of fame, and often also the cause of missing it. A man may lack his due of celebrity from the greater celebrity of his leaders, or of his followers, from his own inability to leave some record of his deeds, or simply from the neglect of historians. But Fortune sometimes plays a particularly unkind trick on the man of parts by sending him into the world at the wrong period of history for him to be appreciated. Such a handicap was attached to Thomas Maule of Panmure, who had the bad luck to be born in 1521 instead of in the reign of George III. In character he belonged to the golden age of field sports. Fate placed him in the turbulent Scotland of the sixteenth century; but, having done so much, provided him also with a son, Commissary Robert Maule, of St Andrews, who has left an admirable account of him.[1]

The Maules were an ancient and distinguished family, of baronial rank in France before the Norman conquest of England, and they had an honourable record in Scotland after their transplanting to this country. More than two hundred years before this Thomas Maule's birth, a Sir Thomas Maule held Brechin Castle for forty days against King Edward I of England. 'When', says a contemporary writer,[2] 'the King of England's mighty catapults hurled stones unceasingly against the walls . . . this Sir Thomas stood with a napkin and rubbed

[1] Printed in the introduction to the *Registrum de Panmure*, 1874.
[2] Matthew of Westminster. See *Wallace Papers*, Maitland Club, 1841, p. 21.

44

off the marks, in scorn and derision of the whole English army.' Unlike Black Agnes in 1338, Sir Thomas Maule performed this ritual once too often, and thereby lost both his life and his castle.

Another Thomas Maule fell at the battle of Harlaw in 1411. In another, who was the great-great-grandfather of the subject of this essay, we find the first evidence of that zest for hunting that distinguished the later Maules; but 'he beine rydand at the huntes neir to the Grein Lawe of Brechin, suddanlie became blind and lost his sight, quharfor he was called the blind knight'. This Sir Thomas was also remarkable for the unusual gesture of divorcing his wife to spite his father-in-law.

His heir was his grandson, yet another Sir Thomas, a pleasant and kindly man. The family temper broke out in him to the extent of his burning 'for ane indignatione' the house of his neighbour John Liddel of Panlathie; but he repented this hasty action, and ultimately allowed Liddel to marry his daughter. He combined piety with good living, providing not only masses for his soul but such meals for his body that, when he fought among his Angus neighbours at Flodden, he was so enormously fat that he literally could not draw his own sword. 'Quhairfor', says the family history, 'the laird of Guthrie drew it furth to him.' Armed at last, but a target no enemy could miss, Sir Thomas fought like his ancestors 'and received many wounds, of which he instantly died in the field'.

Robert Maule, his eldest son and heir, was 'of hie stature, sanguine in coulloure bothe of hyd and haire, colerique of nature, and subject to suddane anger'. Although 'expert in the lawes of the countray' and 'countine of genealogies', he was illiterate, and his signature is always by proxy—'ROBERT MAULE with my hand on the pen'. He was, however, an all-round sportsman—'ane abil man on fut, and ane gud horsman. . . . He had gryt delyght in haukine and hountine. He tuk plesur in playing at the fut bale. . . . Lykwayes he exerciset the gowf, and oftymes past to Barry lynkes,' where sometimes, by a custom not unknown to-day in the same neighbourhood, 'the wadfie [wager] was for drink.' He was, however, 'very temperat of his mouthe,' and if he lost the game did not join the victors at the nineteenth hole, but 'causit ane of his servandis to gange and pay for al'.

We now come to the Thomas Maule whose ancestry has been thus purposely studied. He was the eldest of Robert Maule's fifteen children—few of whom seem to have survived—by his wife Isobel Merser, and was sent to Edinburgh at the age of seven to be educated under 'ane Robert Leslie, quha was ane famous man of lawe in that tyme'. Growing up, he became a favourite of Cardinal Beaton, and was contracted to marry one of his natural daughters. It was King James V who moved Thomas to break off the engagement by the terse advice, 'Marie nevir ane preist's get'. In due course, when he was nearly 25, Thomas married a young widow, Margaret Ogilvy, daughter of George Halyburton of Pitcur. Her first husband, John Ogilvy of Balfour, perished in an outbreak of the plague in Edinburgh, which at that time was 'verey vehement' in all the east coast towns, so that, Bishop Lesley commented, 'it appered weill that God did punische that realme with pleague, weare [war], suord and fyre all at onis for the offences of the peple'.[1]

Margaret was 'ane religious and godly woman', who, according to her son, 'delytit mikil to talk of auld histories, knewe the heal [whole] genealogie of hir father's hous, as also of her mother's, geave meat and drink withe ane mervellous cheirful countenance, luifit al godlie men, detested vice'. Thomas's marriage with her was exceedingly happy; but its beginning lay in a far from tranquil time.

Before he married, Thomas had seen something of war, having been taken prisoner by the English at the battle of Haddon Rig and detained for some time at Morpeth before he was released. He had only been married a few months when he found himself again a soldier and following the Earl of Angus to the muster at Musselburgh where Arran, the Governor of Scotland, had gathered an army, by the unusual means of sending out the fiery cross in the hands of heralds and pur-

[1] *History of Scotland*, Bannatyne Club, 1830, p. 193.

suivants, to repel the Duke of Somerset's invasion of Scotland in September, 1547.

On 10 September Thomas fought with Angus's 'battle' in the disastrous engagement of Pinkie. His division of the army was the right wing or vanguard, and was the first to join action with the English advancing down from Carberry and Falside hill after the impetuous Arran had ordered the Scots to leave their secure position behind the Esk and cross over to intercept the enemy. Thomas stood with the schiltrom of pikemen which repulsed the heavy English cavalry under Lord Grey, which retreated under the fire of the English cannon and hackbuts, and which finally broke in panic-stricken rout in the moment of alarm and uncertainty which caused Arran himself to cry 'Fy, fy! Treason!' and to set his men the example of flight. Thomas's escape from the battlefield provided him with a story to tell for the rest of his life, and its vivid details are preserved in his son's narrative.

After wading the Esk for the second time that day, Thomas halted in his sodden clothes on the far bank to rid himself of the weight of his jack, which he pulled off at length only with difficulty 'by resson he had his purs under his oxter'. Sword in hand and steel bonnet on head, he hurried towards Edinburgh as the pursuing English horse hewed down his comrades. Athletic though he was, he had to rest at last, and 'entrit in the corne yard of Brunstone', where the best refuge he could see was a large cherry-tree, into the thickest of whose branches he climbed for concealment. Two Englishmen brought his heart into his mouth by halting under his tree when 'thear fel fra ane of them sum thinge, bot quhat it wes he could not perseave, bot apperit to be ane purs'—the second time that day that a purse brought his life in jeopardy. The Englishman drew his sword, and 'had mikil ado' to pick up his purse with its point, during which the unhappy Thomas, holding his breath among the branches of the cherry-tree, 'never thought ane tyme so long; bot thearefter, they ridin away, he past to Edinburgh'. Next day, having forgathered with some of his servants, though fourteen of the men he had led to

Musselburgh had been killed, he rode to Queensferry and so won home.

At Panmure, where the news of Pinkie had been before him, Thomas found his father in terrible anxiety. Panmure was not entailed and Margaret was pregnant. 'If scho had been deliverit of ane dauchter, the house sould have gone fra the nam: sa that his father nather did eat nor sleipe, and nan of his domestiques durst almaist com in his presence, for he had ay in mynd the feild of Flodon, quhar his father Sir Thomas was slane, as also the Harlawe, quhar Sir Thomas Maule was slane, and nan of his nam levin on lyf; and except his [Thomas's] wyf had beine deliver of ane sone, the nam had altogidder beine extinguisit; and by and attour this he did bear ane singular luf and favor to his sone.'

Margaret's child proved a boy, but the family's anxieties were not over. The English army advanced to the Tay and took and garrisoned Broughty Castle. At Panmure they captured both Robert and Thomas Maule, and carried them off to imprisonment in England, Robert, who was confined in the Tower of London, being 'evil hurt' by a shot 'in the chaftes' from a culverin. But they both obtained their freedom without ransom, and Robert died peacefully at home in 1560 and was buried beside his wife in the choir of Panbride kirk in a finely carved oak tomb—which by the early eighteenth century was 'almost all broke down'.

After returning from England, Thomas Maule, described by his son as 'ane fair man, of personage lyk to his father, of rudie coullour, his haire read yallowe and his beard, of ane liberal face and blythe countenance, nevir for na adversitie dejected', was able to settle down to the real interests of his life. He took, it seems, little part in public affairs during Queen Mary's reign, though we are told that he was in Aberdeen with the Queen 'befor the slauchter of the Earle of Huntly at Corrichy', and that later he 'followid the factione of the Regents against the Quenis factione'. His taste was for country life and country sports, and he had had enough fighting before he was twenty-six to want no more of it.

His temperament, 'nevir for na adversitie dejected', was undoubtedly a family trait. It appears in a far-off French ancestor, Pierre, Seigneur de Maule, who died in 1106, and who is recorded to have preferred banquets to battles and loathed fasts; in the ironical humour of the defender of Brechin Castle; and in the comfortable living of the stout hero of Flodden. But another trait, the Maule explosion of temper, had lost its force with the years: Thomas was not, like his father, 'colerique of nature'. He inherited his father's red hair and his temperance in drinking, as he inherited the piety of his grandfather and great-grandfather. But unfortunately he did not inherit a head for business. He mismanaged the family estate and sold or alienated a great deal of it, causing much subsequent embarrassment to his eldest son Patrick. He lived only for sport. 'He was ane man not curious of the world, and wald rather suffer loss of gudes than enter in pley with his nychtbouris.'

Hard exercise and the chase were his delights. Like his father, he was 'ane abil man on fut'—as his escape after Pinkie showed. In his young days he and his brother-in-law William Halyburton once walked from Pitcur to the Water of Deane, thence across to the Lunan and so to Panmure, a journey 'estimat thretty myles'. It would have been a notable walk in any case, but the two were also wearing 'jacks' and boots, and each led his horse, on which he had strapped his cloak, and carried a goshawk on his wrist.

Thomas took special pleasure in goshawks and greyhounds. In his youth he even went hawking on Sundays, and even after he gave up this practice because his favourite red tiercel 'brak his winge on ane dyk', he probably continued, after the fashion of the day, to go to church with a hawk on his wrist. Hawking was the favourite sport of country gentlemen, and first-rate hawks were of great value: James IV paid £189 for a trained bird, and in James VI's time a pair of falcons was valued at £2,000.[1] The sport would have appealed strongly to so tireless a pedestrian as Thomas Maule. It was usually followed on foot, and hawking parties did so much damage to

[1] Charles Rogers: *Social Life in Scotland*, 1884, vol. ii, p. 277.

standing crops that in 1555 the Estates passed an Act ordaining 'that na man take upon hand to ryde or gang in their nichtbouris cornes, in halking or hunting, fra the Feast of Pasche [Easter] unto the time that the samin be schorne'.

Hawking engrossed Thomas's mind with a passion only comparable nowadays to the enthusiasm of an angler on a good fishing day. He continued to follow the sport even when he was too old to walk as had been his custom. 'He wald ryd al day . . . fastine, except in the mornings he wald tak ane drink of aile and thearefter ane lytil aquavite, and continewe to the evenings without ather meat or drink, and at his first cumine home at evin wald cal for ane drink. . . . No fair day almaist throwe the heal [whole] yeir bot he was on horsbak, evin in his auld age, except on the Sonday.'

The old sportsman had several chosen companions, mostly relations, of whom the chief 'in his auld age' was John, first Marquis of Hamilton, fourteen years his junior, 'ane nobil man, mekil gevin to the forsaidis exercise, quha honorit him very mikil, sa that he wald com out of Arbrothe to Panmor tymous in the morning, and wald gange upe and downe the hal unto the laird was redy, and his clothes on. He [Hamilton] called him evir "father", and becaus the Marquis usit to hunt with ratches'—dogs hunting by scent—'and the laird with greyhundis, for the respect he buir him wald caus lead the ratches home agane, and only suffer the hundis to rine.'

With the true indifference of the fanatic, Thomas was impervious to any physical discomfort while he hunted or hawked. 'He nevir did ryd withe ane clok, but cot alone, in the cauldest wether in winter, and wald nevir lyght to gang for heat'—that is, walk to get warm—'and cumine to ane watter, quhan as it drew neir evine, wald lyght fra his hors, and in the cauld frost wald wyshe [wash] his haukes' supper, and nevir shrink for cauld, and then cumine home wald cal for ane drink before evir he com to the fyre.'

He died on 7 March 1600, having first 'enterit and confessit his sinnes to God, therefter said the Belief and the Lordis Prayer; quhilk done he willit them al to gange to thear supper in the hal, except ane woman to attend on him, and immediatlie efter they ar set downe his speiche failles him and gevis up the gaist'. His wife, with whom he had lived for more than fifty-three years 'in gryt luif and charite', bore her loss with a Roman fortitude. She 'wald suffer na man nor woman to tuiche him, bot hir self; scho lowked [closed] his eyes and streiked him with ane womanlie countenance and courage, nevir sheddine any teares, bot utterine sum fewe wordis in hir commendations of his honest and luifin hart, albeit I', adds Commissary Maule, 'at the wretin heirof could not do it without gretine.'

Such was Thomas Maule of Panmure. I do not think I exaggerate the charm of his personality, which his son's chronicle so vividly conveys, in claiming that had he been born some two centuries later his name might have become a household word. He was of a type better known, perhaps, among Englishmen than Scotsmen, though it has produced some notable examples in Scotland, such as the second Lord Fife (1729–1809), whose ardour in deer-stalking was at least equal to Maule's in hawking. But, Scotsman or Englishman, had he lived in the golden days of sport and the first great age of biographical portraiture, it is easy to imagine how such a character as his, without the eccentricity of Mytton, but combining the enthusiasm of Squire Osbaldistone with the enduring vitality of Colonel Hawker, would have appealed to such writers as 'Nimrod' and Surtees. And even had he never left Scotland at such a period, Raeburn might have painted him at full length, gun in hand, Kay have sketched his genial countenance, and Burns have celebrated him in such lines as his 'Elegy on Captain Matthew Henderson'. Boswell would have delighted to introduce him to Dr Johnson on their journey northwards to Aberdeen, and Scott to portray him in, perhaps, *The Antiquary*—together with his wife and her taste for 'auld histories'.

4

HERALD AND HISTORIAN:
ALEXANDER NISBET

Tracing genealogies is a hobby no less absorbing to some people than the collection of stamps, porcelain, or autographs to others. Inexplicable, perhaps, to those whom the bug has not bitten, it yet combines some of the thrills of the explorer or the archaeologist with the excitement of trying to solve the mystery of a detective story from which the author has carelessly omitted the conclusion and several of the clues. Its rewards are sometimes more solid than the mere satisfaction of achievement, and may be of value to others besides the researcher himself. The labours, for example, of Mr Aleyn Lyell Reade have added so much to the store of Johnsoniana as to prove genealogy to be not merely an auxiliary but an essential part of biography.

Scholars like Mr Reade are, however, rare, and many genealogists claim to be no more than amateurs. Their tastes in literature, whether professionals or amateurs, are eclectic and peculiar. But into one book which is an essential tool to every Scottish genealogist almost anyone can dip with pleasure—*A System of Heraldry, Speculative and Practical: with the True Art of Blazonry*, published in 1722 by Alexander Nisbet, who has been authoritatively described as 'the ablest and most scientific writer on heraldry in the English language'.

Nisbet has never had a biographer; but a fairly full and extremely readable account of him was prefixed to the publication of some of his 'remains' at the end of the last century and other details are to be found in the Nisbet family history.[1] No portrait of him has been found. But, little though we know of him, what can be gathered concerning his life and character arouses both sympathy and admiration. 'He was,' wrote George Crawfurd, the historian of Renfrewshire, 'a worthy, modest gentleman, who had as many friends and as few enemies as any man I have known.'

Through a series of accidents which will be explained, Nisbet was not a laird, though he should have been. His fame is derived from his writings, and it rests principally on his one major work. This has been injured by an unscrupulous and villainously inaccurate republication of it, several times reprinted, which first appeared in 1742, when he had been seventeen years in his grave, to-day unmarked and unknown, in the Greyfriars kirkyard. The *System of Heraldry* in its original single folio volume only achieved publication three years before its author's death, after years of struggle. Nisbet had been ready to publish his work in 1699, but the expense of printing, and above all of executing the copperplate engravings of armorials which illustrate the book, was beyond his means. He tried to publish by subscription, but could only collect 119 subscribers. He petitioned the Scottish Parliament for a grant in aid, and on the advice of his friends published a short work, *An Essay on Additional Figures and Marks of Cadency*, in 1702 as a specimen of his work and its claims to assistance. By 1704 Parliament's interest had been successfully aroused. They 'were of opinion', wrote Nisbet, 'that something of that nature was very much wanted, and when finished, would be serviceable to the nation: And were so well pleased with my proposals for publishing the same, that the better to enable me thereto, they ordered me two hundred pound sterling, payable out of the tunnage on foreign ships. But that fund not answering their expectations, and being incumber'd with prior assignments, I never had a farthing that way.'

[1] *Alexander Nisbet's Heraldic Plates*, 1892. Introduction by Andrew Ross, Marchmont Herald. See also R. C. Nesbitt: *Nisbet of that ilk*, 1941.

A Parliamentary minute of 1705 explains the disappointment: 'Mr Nisbet's work on herauldry deserves very much to be encouraged, yet the fund of tunnage is either exhausted or embazled.' Nisbet's hopes were finally dashed by the Union of the Parliaments. 'The fund whereout I was to have the money became ineffectual by the Union'; so 'I cooled in the design, and retired for some years to the country.' Before this retreat he witnessed the deposition in Edinburgh Castle of the Scottish Regalia, of which he wrote an exhaustive and valuable account.

Eleven years passed before, in 1718, his next publication appeared—*An Essay on the Ancient and Modern Use of Armories*. This was successful. Times were improving now after the appalling poverty in which Scotland had lain at the beginning of the century, and the country was on the eve of the considerable expansion of commercial and industrial enterprise which began in the last years of George I's reign. A number of Lowland lairds, including some of Nisbet's own friends, had begun the systematic improvement of their estates, and there was, one way and another, much more money in the country than there had been in 1699. There was even a revival of interest in literature, and especially in the history of Scotland: Dr Patrick Abercromby had successfully published his two great folio volumes of *The Martial Atchievements of the Scots Nation* in 1711. Accordingly, Nisbet's *Essay on Armories* had a sale which encouraged him to publish his major work, and this time there were enough supporters for the project to pay for the copper plates, each for the engraving of his own coat-of-arms. The book was handsomely printed, with many pages of armorial 'atchievements', three indexes, a stately dedication to the Duke of Hamilton, and everything fine about it. The preface breathed a dignified exaltation of the author's work:

'I may justly call it an universal system, not calculated for Scotland only, or any particular country, but answering to the regular practice of herauldry through the world. Notwithstanding of which, I may presume to say, that my reader will here find such a collection of armorial bearings of sirnames and families in Scotland, both ancient and modern, that the like was never attempted; and which will serve as a general register, or at least a directory of arms to posterity: a work hitherto much wanted, and earnestly wished for by the curious.'

Alexander Nisbet, in his sixty-fifth year, must have felt a deep satisfaction in turning over the pages of his noble volume, and re-reading the final words of his preface: 'As it is the service of my country, and benefit of posterity, that I chiefly write for, so I shall be easy as to the snarles of idle and ignorant criticks; and shall be ready, on all occasions, fully to satisfy candid and judicious readers; And whatever fate the following book may undergo in the present age, I shall comfort myself with the thoughts of this, That the older it grows, the more useful and valuable will it be to posterity.'

There are no less than seven direct and two indirect appeals to 'posterity' in the four pages of the preface, witnessing to the spirit in which Nisbet had pursued what was in truth a life's work. 'As the study of herauldry is what my peculiar genius[1] has led me to for many years, so I have endeavour'd to adapt my studies that way, to the service of my country.' It was about 1687, as he himself records, that 'having wholly laid aside the imployments of a writer, I applied myself entirely and assiduously to this study'. To the pre-eminence of Nisbet as an authority on heraldry there is sufficient evidence, both ancient and modern. He himself could say proudly of his *Essay on Cadency*: 'It has been approven of by the most knowing heralds in Britain, and particularly by Sir Henry St George, Garter King at Arms, which he was pleased to signify to me in his letter; tho' in it I have shown but a small regard to the English writers in herauldry.' And the opinion of Marchmont Herald in 1892 is unqualified—'As a herald he remains unrivalled.' Oddly enough, however, Nisbet never received, and may never even have been offered, any appointment as a

[1] The word is less boastful than it sounds to a modern ear: it means talent or capacity.

herald or pursuivant. Probably his Jacobite sympathies, of which he made no secret, were regarded as an impediment.

But no reader needs to be a herald to appreciate Nisbet's charm as a writer or the colour and flavour of his prose. He writes intimately, like a man talking, and his frequent endorsement of a blazon with 'I have seen . . .' when citing a particular carving or seal as evidence, carries all the conviction of the first-hand witness. He is generally brief, terse, and to the point, as in his memorable definition—'Arms are silent names'. He himself was conscious that his style was unpretentious for his time. 'I am so much taken up', he wrote, 'in conversing with the dead, and in turning over the works of those who lived many ages before me, that it cannot be expected my writing should appear in that neat dress, into which other modern authors carefully lick themselves.' But it is the very homeliness of his style that makes him so much more readable than some of his contemporaries. Even in his most technical passages he strives for simplicity. It is typical of him to dismiss certain 'needless terms' of the English heralds with the comment—'which I industriously omit, being of no use, but to confuse the blazon, and amuse the reader'.

Yet his approach to his work, as to a high calling and vocation—for 'our ancestors in Scotland . . . never looked on armorial bearings as an idle amusement, but as a matter of great moment and importance to the nation'—gives his style, again and again, a dignity and stateliness all the more effective for the simplicity of his vocabulary. This note is to be heard in the opening of his preface to the *System of Heraldry*:

'The original design of herauldry, is not merely show and pageantry, as some are apt to imagine; but to distinguish persons and families; to represent the heroick atchievements of our ancestors, and to perpetuate their memory; to trace the origin of noble and ancient families, and the various steps by which they arrived at greatness; to distinguish the many different branches descended from the same families; and to show the several relations which one family stands in to another.'

THE HOUSE OF DEAN, NEAR EDINBURGH

(Demolished in 1845)

From a drawing in the National Gallery of Scotland

It appears again in his reproof of popular inattention to heraldry:

'I cannot sufficiently wonder at the vanity of a great many, who glory in their carrying these marks and signs of honour, which they do not at all understand, and must regret it in the greatest part of my countrymen, who, tho' otherwise well qualified in the knowledge of other liberal arts and sciences, yet neglect to apply themselves to the study of herauldry; a science so valuable, that the greatest men in all ages have thought it worth their study and application.'

These sustained passages are rare, but they are further testimony to Nisbet's earnestness in his work. His attitude towards it was scientific rather than in any way romantic. Much of his reputation among experts rests on his being the first writer to treat of heraldry realistically and wholly histori-cally, eschewing all such vagaries as tracing its origins back to the siege of Troy or earlier, and trying to blazon the arms of Joshua, Duke of Israel, or Judas Maccabaeus. 'Antiquaries, historians, and heraulds', he says, 'amuse us with many various forms of shields used by the ancients, which are but of little use to us, therefore I shall be very brief with 'em.' As straightforward as his definition of 'the original design of herauldry', and as nobly expressed, is his purpose 'to flatter no man, but fairly and truly to collect from authentick documents, seals, tombs, and other monuments, whatsoever may tend to the honour of the King and country in general, and what may be for the advantage and satisfaction of many private families, whose worthy and generous ancestors once in a day made as great a figure in the world as their now opulent neighbours'.

The general reader, even if less interested in heraldry for its own sake as 'no less useful than curious' than Nisbet would desire him to be, can find ample pleasure in the fantastic vocabulary of the subject, and in chasing through the pages of the *System* the discussion of bends and besants, baronets' badges and borders gobonated; or—dipping into other sections of the heraldic index—lions passant guardant, lymphads and lozenges; or tierces, toads, towers and trefoils. Even more romantic are the almost astrological virtues of heraldic beasts, summarised in Nisbet's stateliest manner. The unicorn, for instance, 'is of great esteem . . . remarkable for his strength, but more for his great and haughty mind, who would rather die than be brought to subjection'. The boar 'is a champion among other wild-beasts, and encounters his enemy with a noble courage. . . . He betokeneth a man of a bold spirit, skillful and politick in warlike fates' (a word which Nisbet uses for 'feats'). The elephant is 'commended for his good qualities, and as the emblem of wit, docility, and meekness'; while the swan, 'a bird of great beauty and strength', is 'the symbol of a learned man, and of one that knows best how to contemn the world, and to die with resolution'.

The *System of Heraldry* is full of such musical passages. But another of its engaging qualities is its innumerable digressions into matters which are not heraldic but historical. Nisbet was an historian *manqué*. He frequently gives the history of a family at length, and sometimes records details available nowhere else. Several times he prints in full the text of a royal letter directing a grant of arms, such as that of King James V granting to John Scott of Thirlestane a specially honourable augmentation to his armorial bearings for 'comand to our host at Soutra Edge with threescore and ten launciers on horseback, of his friends and followers. And', adds this pathetic letter, written only a few months before the disaster of Solway Moss, 'beand willing to gang with us into England, when all our nobles and others refused, he was ready to stake all at our bidding.'

Besides these detailed records, the *System of Heraldry* is rich in brief anecdotes illustrative of armorial bearings. Some are well known: those, for example, of the hay waggon of Binning, the shakefork of Cunningham, and the dagger crest and motto 'I'll make sure' of Kirkpatrick of Kilosburn, derived from that Roger Kirkpatrick who 'was one of the first that stood up for the interest of King Robert the Bruce' and 'in the church of Dumfries . . . gave Cumming several stobs with a dagger'. Others, of more dubious authenticity, Nisbet records

with a judicious scepticism. He expresses no doubts of Sir
James Douglas's having carried the Bruce's heart on crusade,
and that journey's commemoration by 'a man's heart gules'
on the Douglas shield, though he makes it quite clear that 'the
ancient arms of the Douglasses were azure, three stars argent
which, it seems, were altered'. But his tone is more hesitant in
alluding to the companion family legend of the Lockharts.
'This family, it seems, of old carried azure, three boars' heads
erazed, within a border ingrailed or, as in Balfour's and Pont's
MSS. One of the heads of this family is said by some'—Nisbet
plainly does not endorse the story—'to have accompanied
good Sir James Douglas, with King Robert the Bruce's heart,
to Jerusalem. The family have since altered their arms, either
to perpetuate the same story, or to make their arms more uni-
vocal to the name.' He shows that the name was Loccard in
the reign of Malcolm IV, though 'now writ Lockhart'—a form
which in fact was not known before 1637.[1]

Nisbet allows himself more irony in referring to the national
flag. 'A Saltier (or St Andrew's Cross) argent . . . has been
antiently used by the Scots for their ensign, upon as well
grounded a tradition for its appearing in the air, as other
nations have for their crosses coming down from heaven.'

Many other stories and allusions, however, seem to have been
included for little reason but the mere pleasure of recording
them, such as the motto on the Kincaid broadsword, dated 1552:

Wha will persew, I will defend
My life and honour to the end.

Similarly pointless but delightful is the curious anecdote of Sir
Francis Leke of Sutton, afterwards Earl of Scarsdale:

'He was eminently loyal; and his two sons were killed in the
King's service: and having himself suffered much for his
loyalty in these ruinous times, he became so much mortified
(as the English observe) after the murder of his rightful sovereign Charles I that he apparelled himself in sack-cloath, and
causing his grave to be dug some years before his death, laid

[1] See Dr George F. Black's *The Surnames of Scotland*, 1947.

himself down in it every Friday, exercising himself in divine meditations and prayers.'

Frequently an admiring epithet or a phrase or two of eulogy testify to Alexander Nisbet's respect for this or that family's record in the history of Scotland. He shows special favour towards families which were, like the main branch of his own, Royalist and anti-Covenanter in the preceding century, and several allusions show his reverence for the memory of Montrose, 'who, with a small army for the King, did fates beyond belief against the Covenanters'. His political sympathies colour some of his descriptions, as when he designates that formidable harrier of the Covenanters, General Thomas Dalyell of the Binns, 'a loyal gentleman' who 'was suitably honoured by a canton argent, charged with a sword and pistol saltierways gules, to show his honourable employment.' Such phrases would have caused some eyebrows to rise or to contract even as late as 1722.

But even the stubbornest Cameronian might have forgiven Nisbet such partiality for the patriotic fervour with which he records less controversial service to King and country. Most of his narrative digressions are into 'fates' in battle by bygone Scottish champions. In more than twenty cases he goes out of his way to chronicle the death of ancestors 'in the unfortunate field of Flowden'. But the most striking of all his digressions, for its disproportionate length—more than one and a half folio pages—is his enthusiastic description of how Colonel Alexander Campbell of Finnab in Perthshire won his augmentation of arms. It was on account of his victory over a Spanish force at Toubacanti in Darien on 5 February 1700 that Colonel Campbell was granted, 'by way of distinction', the arms of the Company of Scotland to add to his own.[1] 'I hope', Nisbet apologises, 'the reader will excuse my being so particular in this narration, which I could not avoid, without being unjust to the valour of the man, and to the gratitude of our countrymen.'

It was only natural that antiquarian interest, pride of race,

[1] Another version of this thrilling tale is given in Dr G. P. Insh's *The Company of Scotland*, 1932, pp. 189–192.

and admiration for military valour should combine in an equally long account of the author's own family, the Nisbets of that ilk. But here there comes to light the chief disappointment of Nisbet's life, greater even than the long frustration he endured before the ultimate publication of his *System of Heraldry*. Alexander Nisbet was, as he wistfully records, 'the only male represener' of his ancient line, but he had lost the family inheritance. He was a landless man: a laird by birth but not by possession.

The Nisbets of that ilk were an old Berwickshire family going back to the twelfth century. Alexander's grandfather and namesake, who in 1630 had rebuilt the old castle, two miles from Duns, as 'the House of Nisbet', had 'strenuously opposed the Covenanters; but they prevailing, he and his sons were forced to leave the country, and join with the King's army, where they served in honourable posts with valour and untainted loyalty, to the loss of their persons and estate.' The eldest son, Sir Philip Nisbet, was taken prisoner at Philiphaugh and executed at Glasgow. 'Alexander and Robert, both captains, were killed in the field, following Montrose. Mr John the fourth son married, and died in England'; while Adam, the youngest, 'married Janet Aikenhead, grandchild to David Aikenhead, Provost of Edinburgh, father and mother of the author of this *System of Heraldry* who is the only male represener of the ancient and honourable family of Nisbet.'[1]

The cause of Nisbet's disinheritance was not political but prosaically financial. Old Sir Alexander, deep in debt, had resisted his creditors, defying or eluding all legal processes and several Acts of Parliament, for many years, but at length, in 1652, executed a disposition of his estate in favour of John Ker, merchant burgess in Edinburgh, brother of Sir Thomas Ker of Cavers, who took it on himself to satisfy the other creditors and made a not ungenerous allowance for the maintenance of Sir Alexander and his surviving family.

[1] But the line of his great-grandfather, Sir Philip Nisbet of that ilk, continued through his second son.—R. C. Nesbitt: *Nisbet of that ilk*, 1941, p. 20, note.

After the Restoration, however, Sir Alexander considered that the reward of his loyalty should be the return of his lands, and petitioned the Scottish Parliament accordingly. As justice was clearly not on his side, wherever sympathies may have lain, his suit was dismissed, and the Nisbet lands remained in the possession of Lord Sinclair, the lineal representative of the purchaser.

Considering the difficulty that Sir Alexander's creditors had had to secure their rights, it was not surprising that the title-deeds of the Nisbet estate were most jealously preserved. Hence the slippery tactics of Sir Alexander recoiled on the head of his grandson when he came to write up the Nisbet history for the *System of Heraldry*. 'What I shall say of this ancient and honourable family in general', he wrote sadly, 'is not without documents, which are to be seen among the records of Durham, Priory of Coldinghame, Abbacy of Kelso, and other chartularies; but from the charter-chest of the family, which I suppose is in the custody of the present possessors of these lands, I cannot avouch any thing, never having had access thereto.' Thus the sadness of the dispossessed heir was blended with the regret of the conscientious historian; and the last of the Nisbets of that ilk could only describe himself on the title-pages of his books as 'Alexander Nisbet, Gent.'

He died on 5 December 1725 in the ancient castle of Dirleton, and was buried two days later in the Greyfriars kirkyard in Edinburgh. The register, which describes him as 'Alexander Nisbet, Professor of Herauldrie', records that his body was laid 'close to the south side of Nisbet's tomb', but the exact spot is unknown.[1] The old House of Dean, within whose walls Nisbet is traditionally supposed to have written his *System of Heraldry*, stands no longer, having been demolished when the Dean Cemetery was laid out in 1845.[2] A tablet in the Greyfriars kirk, erected at the expense of his kinsman Mr Robert Chancellor Nesbitt and unveiled by John Buchan in 1934, commemorates his life, death and burial. But his immortal memorial, beyond a doubt, is his book.

[1] Nesbitt, *op. cit.*, p. 147.   [2] *Ibid.*, pp. 23–4.

5

CROSBIE AND THE CRAUFURDS

If Alexander Nisbet was a laird without an estate, Crosbie, near West Kilbride in the Cunningham district of Ayrshire, is to-day an estate without a laird. Alternatively, however, it might be described as a diminished estate with over 30,000 lairds, for the old house and the surrounding policies now belong to the Scottish Youth Hostels Association. It was on a windy day of sun and showers in July, 1947, that Crosbie entered on this last phase of its long history, a day of music and merriment, with the old house packed to its roof-tree. Some may regret the transformation of an old family home into a youth hostel. Others may rejoice that so pleasant and interesting a building should remain, as a home should be, a centre of hospitality and happiness, and should become a means of educating thousands of young Scots in the appreciation of their country's history, culture and craftsmanship. But both schools of thought can agree in the satisfactory reflection that Crosbie, unlike many other old houses, is now safe from either demolition or commercial exploitation. It survives and will survive as the last monument of an old but now extinct family, the Craufurds of Crosbie and Auchenames, from whom it was anciently known, to distinguish it from another Crosbie in Kyle, as 'Crosbie-Craufurd'.[1]

The pedigree of the Craufurds can be traced down through some 600 years, but remarkably little is known about more than a few of them. This is chiefly due to an accident of the

[1] *New Statistical Account of Scotland* (West Kilbride), vol. v, p. 254.

eighteenth century to which I shall allude later. Their story begins in the thirteenth century, and its tradition was thus recorded about 1608 by the cartographer and antiquarian Timothy Pont:

'Corsby-toure is the habitatione of William Craufurd of Achnaims by divers thought to be c[h]eiffe of the Craufurds, he holdes the same of the Earls of Glencairne. This surname is verry ancient and did memorable service under K. Alexander the 3d at the batell of Largis by quhome ther good service was nobly recompensed with divers grate lands and possessiones.'[1]

But the first of the family of whom there is contemporary record was Sir Reginald Craufurd of Crosbie, second son of Hugh Craufurd of Loudoun, who had in 1320 a grant of the barony of Auchenames in Renfrewshire from King Robert I, as well as an augmentation to his arms of two lances in saltire in commemoration of his exploits at Bannockburn. Heralds disagree as to the blazonry of the augmented coat, whether it was 'argent, two spears saltire-ways, between four spots of ermine' or 'gules, a fess ermine surmounted of two launces in saltire argent'.[2] There is even more uncertainty about the visit of William Wallace, 'in Corsby for to bide' for sixteen days of one August when the English were hot on his heels—a tale which rests on no evidence but that of Blind Harry. But at least the succession of the family from Sir Reginald Craufurd's time onward is clear.

The fourth generation from Sir Reginald brings us to Robert Craufurd of Auchenames, whose youngest son, also called Robert, fell, like so many other Ayrshiremen, at Flodden,[3] and was succeeded by his eldest son, James, who had had a charter of Crosbie from him in 1498. James's son Thomas, the next laird, survives in two records, neither of them to his credit. He

[1] *Cuninghame, topographized by Timothy Pont, A.M.*, 1604–8, ed. J. S. Dobie, 1876, p. 113.

[2] Alexander Nisbet: *A System of Heraldry*, 1722, pp. 56–7.

[3] The Renfrewshire historian George Crawfurd erroneously made the elder Robert the one who was killed at Flodden. Crawfurd's *General Description of the Shire of Renfrew*, ed. Robertson, 1818, p. 81; cf. Paterson's *Ayrshire: Cunningham*, p. 324.

was one of a large band who, headed by two grandsons of the
Earl of Glencairn, were accused of lying in wait, 'umbesetting
the highway,' with intent to murder William, Lord Sempill, in
August, 1533. This, however, may testify to no more than
Auchenames's solidarity in a popular cause, for Lord Sempill
had been suspected, only a few months before, of having been
art and part in the murder of William Cunynghame of Craig-
ends, a cadet of the house of Glencairn, and his acquittal had
been regarded by the dead man's son and others as 'manifest
and wilfull errour'.[1]

But no excuse seems possible for Thomas Craufurd when he
was again in conflict with the law five years later. He was
accused, with one accomplice, of abducting and imprisoning a
chaplain, his namesake, at Auchenames; with another of evict-
ing a widow and her son from a small holding on the Auchenames estate; and with both, and his brother James, of 'the
cruel slaughter and murder of John Quhite, committed of fore-
thought felony'.[2]

Thomas Craufurd died in 1541, and after him his three sons,
John, William and Patrick, were successively the owners of the
family property. John was killed at Pinkie in 1547, leaving no
children. William, who lived till 1582, left a son, James Craufurd of Crosbie, who in turn left a daughter and heiress named
Jean.[3] Patrick, who does not seem to have long survived
William, left Auchenames to his son, another William, the same
who once welcomed to Crosbie the wandering Timothy Pont.

At this point the succession to Crosbie turned upon a story
which, although only briefly hinted at in the records, seems to
hold all the ingredients of a remarkable romance.

Jean Craufurd is said to have been 'the heiress of Crosbie',[4]
but it seems more likely that that was rather what she wished

[1] Robert Pitcairn: *Criminal Trials in Scotland*, 1833, vol. i, pp.
164, 165–7.
[2] *Ibid.*, p. 205.
[3] So named by Crawfurd, *op. cit.*, p. 82; Robertson and Paterson
refine her into Jane.
[4] Crawfurd's *Renfrewshire, ut cit.*, p. 370.

to be, and that in reality it passed on her father's death to his first cousin William, the laird of Auchenames. Such is the implication of Pont's definite statement, written in William's lifetime—'Corsby-toure is the habitatione of William Craufurd of Achnaims. . . . He holds the same of the Earls of Glencairn.' Whatever the legal position, Jean Craufurd, who seems to have been a strong-minded young woman, achieved her desire to retain Crosbie as her home. She determined to marry no one but her second cousin Patrick, William's son and thus the heir to Auchenames, if not to Crosbie also. The difficulty in the way of this plan was that Patrick was, in the words of the song, 'ower young to marry yet', being in fact ten years younger than Jean. However, she 'reserved herself'[1] for her cousin, and married him in 1606, when he was 18 and she 28.

Thus the two families of Craufurd of Crosbie and Craufurd of Auchenames were once more conjoined. William Craufurd lived till 1613, and Patrick and Jean then settled down to a long and, for all we know to the contrary, a happy married life at Crosbie. They had six sons and two daughters. Patrick lived till 1649, and was survived by Jean, the date of whose death I have not discovered.

It was these two, in all probability, who pulled down 'Corsby-toure' and built the house which forms the older portion of the modern Crosbie. It is true that the initials of the monogram carved on three separate places of the building are those of their grandson Archibald Craufurd and his wife Margaret Porterfield. But the dates accompanying these monograms, of which the earliest is 1676, all differ, and seem to record the periods of various alterations and improvements to an existing building. The style of the old part of Crosbie, which was a gabled oblong of three stories and an attic, with a projecting staircase tower making the whole a T-shaped building, compares suggestively with that of several other erections of the time of Charles I: Patrick's period, not Archibald's. The whole appearance of the house strongly recalls that of a wing of Penkill, near Old Dailly in Carrick, which was added in 1628.

[1] Crawfurd's *Renfrewshire*.

There are also points of resemblance with Peffermill and Saughton Mills, both near Edinburgh, and Brisbane (now destroyed) near Largs; Saughton Mills dates from 1623 and the other two from 1636. Apart from this architectural evidence, it is usually the generation with a large number of children that feels the urge to pull down the family home and rebuild it; and Patrick and Jean had eight children, their eldest son William only one and their grandson Archibald only four.

William Craufurd and his wife Anna Lamont are again very shadowy figures. Their son Archibald seems to have been of the stirring type. He favoured the Covenanting cause, and on 30 July 1683 was imprisoned 'on suspicion of being concerned in the affair of Bothwell Brig', but was afterwards released. Like most of his ancestors, he married a Renfrewshire girl, Margaret Porterfield; and he and his wife give an impression of restlessness by the number of times they made alterations to the house. The exact nature of their operations is uncertain: perhaps they added the dormer windows and the cosy little watch-room, with its fireplace and the window looking towards the sea, which caps the staircase tower. Anyway, they were moved to inscribe their monogram on the house as a record in 1676 (the year in which Archibald was retoured heir to his father), in 1680 and once again in 1687.

Margaret died after bearing four children. The only son, William, was married to a niece of Bishop Burnet, but on his early death, in 1695, left only one daughter, named Helen. 'On which', says the family history, 'his father, unwilling that his estates should pass from the family through a female, married, secondly, a lady of the family of Shaw Stewart of Greenock, but was in this disappointed, for by this lady he had no issue.' He died in 1715.

Once again, as over a century before, the Craufurd succession to Crosbie was like to fail; but once again it was saved through the marriage of a Patrick and a Jean. This Patrick was the last representative of another of the many Craufurd families in the west of Scotland, Craufurd of Drumsoy, which descended from an older one which had long flourished on the banks of the Doon, Craufurd of Kerse. Patrick Craufurd was a merchant in Edinburgh and had made a comfortable fortune, so that, having married Archibald Craufurd's second daughter, Jean, he was able to step in when 'the estates of Auchenames and Crosbie were brought to judicial sale in 1715'[1] and buy them, thus becoming a multiple laird with a whole string of territorial titles. Patrick Craufurd of Auchenames, Crosbie, Kerse and Drumsoy had an even better claim than his ancestor, the William Craufurd whom Pont knew, to be called 'cheiffe of the Craufurds'. Another version of his acquisition of Crosbie and Auchenames is that 'Jane, the second daughter, having married the male representative of the other families . . . derived all, as there is every reason to believe, from the same original stock, an arrangement was made by which the estates of Corsbie and Achinames were retained to her and her husband (who, in a judicial proceeding, was decerned and ordained as heir male of Archibald and William).'[2]

Patrick lived till 1733 and Jean till 1740. They had a large family—seven sons and two daughters—and Patrick had four other children by an earlier marriage; but only three of their posterity concern the story of Crosbie—Patrick, Jean's eldest son, who went into Parliament, George, the second, who became a soldier and died lieutenant-colonel of the 53rd regiment of foot, and Ronald, the third, who settled in Edinburgh and became a Writer to the Signet.

This next Patrick, who died in 1778, is a much less shadowy figure than his ancestors, for letters of his often turn up in Scottish family archives. He was known to his friends as 'Peter' and was evidently much liked. This popularity, and his complete subservience to Lord Bute and Lord Bute's uncle, the third Duke of Argyll, probably account—for he seems to have shown no political ability—for his being chosen Member of Parliament for Ayrshire in 1741 and 1747. As such he was regarded with respect, and was one of the correspondents to whom the Provost of Glasgow wrote accounts of that city's

[1] Burke's *Landed Gentry*.
[2] Crawfurd's *Renfrewshire*, p. 371, followed by Paterson, p. 325.

anxieties during the Jacobite rising of 1745.[1] In 1761 he became M.P. for Renfrewshire.

He was twice married, having a daughter by his first wife and two sons, John and James, by his second.

Patrick's brother, Colonel George Craufurd, is only important in the family history as the grandfather of a later laird of Crosbie. The third brother, Ronald Craufurd of Restalrig, W.S., was involved in a misfortune which affected the family as well as himself. He evidently acted as the family lawyer; and in his small apartments in one of the high lands off the High Street of Edinburgh kept all the accumulated charters and other documents of the Craufurds of Kerse, Drumsoy, Auchinames and Crosbie to whom his father had fallen heir. These were not the only archives in his custody, for he enjoyed a flourishing business as 'doer' for various landed families. The whole collection was lost in a disastrous fire which raged among the packed tenements of the Old Town on 9 May 1741. Another writer, James Nasmyth of Earlshall, described the mischief in a letter three days later:

'The fire on Saturday hath done incredible damneage. The insureance on the houses burnt downe amounts to 2600 *l.* sterling, damnage to furniture, &c. to many thousands more, besides losses that are not to be repaired. Ronald Craufurd, Wryter to the Signet, doer for Lord Selkirk, Lord Dair and a great many more people of distinctione, hath lost all his papers of immense value and scarce got out with life. Consul Pringle, Mr Murray one of the principall clerks [of Session], and a good many more have lost all. The Parliament House and New Church [part of St Giles's] were filled with furniture from the familys who judged it necessary for them to move. In short there was nothing but a horror and confusione the whole toun over, so terrible apeareance the flames made. But this is too dismall a scene to dwell on.'[2]

---

[1] *The Cochrane Correspondence*, Maitland Club, 1836, pp. 26–32, 62–4.

[2] James Nasmyth of Earlshall to Alexander Murray of Broughton, 12 May 1741: Broughton MSS, in the possession of Mrs Murray-Usher.

This accident accounts for the fragmentary nature of the Craufurd family history.

In 1764 Patrick Craufurd feued out the whole of the family estate of Auchenames in Renfrewshire, retaining only the 'superiority' of it—the right to vote in Parliamentary elections as a freeholder in the county. The family had not lived at Auchenames for generations. Early in the century it had been described as 'neglected . . . ane old towr house, and no great improvement about it',[1] and by 1795 it was 'demolished almost to the foundation',[2] so that there was no reason beyond sentiment for retaining it. A more positive reason for raising money from the Auchenames estate was the heavy expense which Craufurd had incurred by his election contests in Ayrshire. Although direct bribery of voters was not common in Scottish county elections in the eighteenth century, Craufurd was one of the few, and one of the earliest, to employ it. There is a contemporary comment on his doings during the General Election of 1754 in a letter to John, fourth Earl of Loudoun, whose candidate won the Ayrshire seat in that contest. 'I understand', wrote Allan Whitefoord of Ballochmile, 'my friend Crawfurd is playing his golden engine against you and with some success but it will not avail him in the main.'[3]

Despite his political expenditure, Craufurd looked after the Crosbie estate with care, adding to it in 1737 the lands of Portincross on the coast near West Kilbride, and at some other date the neighbouring estate of Arneil. Like other Ayrshire lairds of this time, he enclosed and improved his lands, but his successors did not carry on his work and his arable lands lapsed into pasture.[4] It was probably he, too, who planted the

[1] William Hamilton of Wishaw: *Accompt of the Sheriffdom of Ranfrew*, c. 1710, Maitland Club, 1831, p. 103.

[2] *Statistical Account of Scotland* (Kilbarchan), vol. xv, p. 489, note. 'The last vestige of the old Auchinames castle was barbarously erased by a new proprietor, to make way for his new house, within these two years.'—*Paisley Magazine*, 2 June 1828, p. 316.

[3] *Scottish Historical Review*, vol. xxvi, p. 130.

[4] *New Statistical Account of Scotland* (West Kilbride), vol. v, p. 255, note.

fine tall beeches that still stand in the glen just below the house.

He stood for the Renfrewshire Parliamentary seat again in 1768, but withdrew before the election on condition that William MacDowall of Castlesemple, who was elected, should support his son John, at this time M.P. for Old Sarum, as a candidate for Renfrewshire at the next General Election.[1] Patrick Craufurd seems to have passed the last few years of his life at Bath. He was by then something of an invalid, and not on the best of terms with his son John, who wrote unsympathetically of him to an old family friend, William Mure of Caldwell, in 1773:

'He is much as you saw him in Scotland, but with the additional misfortune of being almost constantly deaf. Add to this, that his temper or his mind are quite gone. He is grown anxious and attentive to money matters beyond what I ever saw an example of in anybody. I have been wearied by his persecutions into an entail of my estate along with his, which I know I shall repent all the rest of my life.'[2]

In a later letter, too, there is a reference to 'my father, whose illness makes him not altogether so accurate as he used to be'.[3]

The father's side of this unhappy relationship is stated with some pathos in a letter to John Craufurd from a distinguished man who was a friend of both—David Hume. Writing from Edinburgh on 28 January 1774, he says:

'I was told yesterday by Mr Ross[4] that he had just come from your father, who regretted very feelingly his never hearing from you. . . . In the fullness of his heart he . . . declared that, except a reasonable provision for your sister, and a small annuity to your brother after purchasing his commission, he intended you to be the sole heir of all his remaining property. He wanted nothing from you except your friendship, which he was very sorry he could not obtain,

---

[1] *Caldwell Papers*, 1885, Part II, vol. ii, pp. 135–7.
[2] *Ibid.*, pp. 216–7.   [3] *Ibid.*, p. [237].
[4] David Ross (1727–1805), afterwards Lord Ankerville.

and it was the circumstance that embittered his remaining days. . . .'[1]

The picture of John Craufurd of Auchenames and Crosbie, as he became on his father's death in 1778, which this letter reflects is not attractive. Yet if his character was hardly admirable, it certainly had its likable aspects. John never married, and died in 1814. Like his father, he spent a good many years in Parliament, as member for Old Sarum, an English rotten borough (1768–74), for Renfrewshire (1774–80), and for the Glasgow group of burghs (1780–4, and for a few months in 1790). He did not take a very serious view of his Parliamentary duties, regarding the House of Commons chiefly as a rather pleasant club. Nor do his contemporaries seem to have taken him very seriously as a politician, as a letter of 1784 shows, discussing prospective Parliamentary candidates for Ayrshire. 'Craufurd', says the writer, 'is in every way an improper man, except in one respect, that he would vote right. H. Montgomery is an improper man for the only reason that Craufurd is proper, viz. that he would vote wrong.'[2]

Another letter of the same year, written by John Craufurd's friend, Thomas Coutts the banker, is even more flippant:

'Jack Crawford seems to bear his disappointments pretty well, but I dare say he will pay his way into Parliament the first opportunity that offers. It is the fashion to be there and those he lives with are in it. He should buy a seat always, for his indolence will never do to keep up an interest even in a county.'[3]

Among the London society in which Craufurd spent much of his time he was known as 'The Fish'. This may have been from something in his appearance, but I am more inclined to

[1] *The Letters of David Hume*, ed. J. Y. T. Greig, 1932, vol. ii, pp. 283–4.

[2] William Adam to Thomas Kennedy of Dunure, 22 March 1784 (Dunure MSS, in the possession of Lieut.-Col. J. K. MacFarlan of Dunure).

[3] E. H. Coleridge: *The Life of Thomas Coutts, Banker*, 1920, vol. i, p. 184.

think that it was from his easy-going ways—he always swam
with the stream. The Duke of Queensberry burst out in an
explosion of temper and shook his fist in Craufurd's face when
'The Fish' once presumed to doubt if the Duke was expressing
his 'genuine sentiments'; and someone who heard of the incident remarked, 'I do not wonder that any man should be
angry at having his sincerity in political opinions questioned
by *Crawford*.'[1]

George Selwyn had a violent dislike for Fish Craufurd, and
tells several stories against him in his letters, of which the
usual theme is Craufurd's desire to be well with both sides in
politics—'He votes with those who are in, and loves cordially
those who are out.'[2] The most entertaining of these anecdotes
refers to a period just after Lord North's dismissal from office
in 1782:

'The Fish told Lord N. the other night, after the division,
that he had only three bottles left of that champagne which he
liked so much, and if he would come and dine with him they
were at his service. Lord North replied, archly enough, "What!
still, Mr Craufurd, may I dine with you?" '[3]

It is clear, however, that all these stories are prejudiced; and
it is quite possible that the Fish's pliability, in an age when,
after all, party differences were not bitter, arose really from a
general friendliness to all men. Against his ill-wishers may be
set a very respectable list of friends. He was one of Fox's
intimates. Earlier, as '*le petit Craufurd*', he was a familiar
figure in Mme du Deffand's salon, where began his friendship
with Horace Walpole.[4] David Hume went out of his way to
oblige 'Jack';[5] and Gibbon referred to him as 'the hospitable
Craufurd', and had a 'particular regard' for him. Craufurd was,
indeed, one of the last to see Gibbon alive, spending two hours

---

[1] James Hare to Lord Carlisle, 11 Feb. 1782: *Historical MSS
Commission, Carlyle Papers*, p. 576.

[2] George Selwyn to Lord Carlisle, 25 Nov. 1775: *ibid.*, p. 749.

[3] Selwyn to Carlisle: *ibid.*, p. 600.

[4] R. W. Ketton-Cremer: *Horace Walpole*, 1940, pp. 260, 264.

[5] *Caldwell Papers*, Part II, vol. ii, pp. 216, 236, 237–8, 241.

with him in conversation on the day before his death.[1] Some
years later he is recorded as a guest at Holland House,[2] where
he was no doubt as good company as he evidently was in
Brooks's. There is, in fact, plenty of evidence to show that he
was a likable man, full of good humour and, if he is the 'Mr
Crawfurd' quoted by Mrs Thrale,[3] not devoid of wit.

Neither John nor the other two children of Patrick Craufurd
left any descendants. James, a colonel in the Brigade of
Guards, died unmarried in 1811 as Governor of Bermuda,
where his half-sister Sarah had also died in 1796. (Her name—
'Miss Craufurd of Auchinames'—appears in the list of subscribers to the first Edinburgh edition of Burns's poems in
1787.)

On the death of 'The Fish', therefore, Crosbie passed to his
first cousin once removed, another John Craufurd, grandson of
Colonel George Craufurd, the brother of Patrick and Ronald.
He married, in the year of his predecessor's death, 1814, a
great-granddaughter of Sir Robert Walpole—Sophia Mari-
anna, daughter of Major-General Horace Churchill. They had
four sons and two daughters.

Crosbie seems to have been rather neglected during the lifetime of this owner, who died in 1866, and of his son and successor, Edward Henry John Craufurd (1816–87), who was
Member of Parliament for the Ayr burghs from 1852–74. By
Victorian standards it was a small and cramped house, not
very suitable for entertaining numbers of guests and giving
large dinner-parties, as was then the fashion. Not being a
mediaeval building and having nothing of the castle about it—
though it was grandiosely styled 'Crosbie Castle' in Edward
Craufurd's time—it would have little appeal to the contemporary taste for spurious Gothic. It appears that the family
did not inhabit Crosbie, but from time to time, as though

[1] Gibbon's *Memoirs of my Life and Writings*, ed. G. Birkbeck
Hill, 1900, pp. 260, 265.

[2] Lord Ilchester: *The Home of the Hollands*, 1605–1820, 1937,
pp. 199–200.

[3] *Thraliana*, ed. Katharine C. Balderston, 1942, p. 236.

pricked by conscience, kept it in repair. It had been described in 1820 as 'in good preservation, though not habitable'.[1]

The 'New Statistical Account' of West Kilbride, published in 1845, says of the Crosbie estate: 'There is a small mansion-house on it . . . which was long ruinous, but is now being restored in good taste by the proprietor.'[2] The second edition of James Paterson's *History of the County of Ayr*, published in 1863, says:

'The proper seat of the family is Corsbie Castle—it has been made habitable, and is now used as a shooting-box; but they possess a neat cottage residence in the immediate vicinity of the old Castle of Portincross, which is also their property.'[3]

In 1874 the editor of Timothy Pont recorded of Crosbie that 'when undergoing some still more recent repairs, it narrowly escaped destruction by fire. It is now in good preservation, tenanted by the forester, and occasionally occupied as shooting quarters. Its fine old woods make it a favourite resort for pleasure parties.'[4]

Five years after the death of Edward Craufurd, and during the brief ownership of his son, Hugh Ronald George Craufurd, the last of the Craufurds of Crosbie, a short account of the house appeared in the great work of MacGibbon and Ross, with a drawing of the building which is of special interest since it shows Crosbie as it was before modern additions and alterations sadly altered its character. 'For many years', wrote these authors, 'the house was empty and uncared for, though not ruinous, but within the last two or three years it has been put in good repair.'[5]

This expert account of Crosbie singles out for special description the 'curiously placed window' on the second floor, the 'handsome greystone fireplaces, with lintels and jambs deeply

[1] George Robertson: *Topographical Description of Cunninghame*, 1820, p. 130.
[2] *New Statistical Account of Scotland*, vol. v, p. 254.
[3] Paterson's *Ayrshire; Cunningham*, p. 326.
[4] *Cuninghame, topographized by Timothy Pont*, p. 114.
[5] David MacGibbon and Thomas Ross: *The Castellated and Domestic Architecture of Scotland*, vol. iv (1892), p. 119.

moulded at the sides and a flat surface between', the arched
fireplace in the dining-room, the oak shutters and linings of the
window recesses, carved in a simple but effective diamond
pattern, and the well preserved wheel-stair in the tower, all
of which survive to-day. The accompanying drawing indicates
also a panel over the old entrance doorway (now made into a
window) which probably contained a coat-of-arms. Whether
this was the old coat of the Craufurds according to Sir James
Balfour of Denmiln, Lyon King of Arms to Charles I and
Charles II—'Gules, a fess ermine surmounted by two lances
in saltire argent'—or the device 'Argent, two spears saltire-
ways between four spots of ermine' borne by the eighteenth
century Craufurds of Auchenames and Crosbie, it is now impossible to say. To-day a crest occupies the same place: an arm
holding a spear, with the motto '*Pro Rege*'.

This crest has nothing to do with the Craufurds but is that
of James Graham, LL.D., who in 1896 bought Crosbie from
Hugh Craufurd, who afterwards settled in Canada, and built a
large modern wing on to the house, thus altering the T-shape
into an L. The additions altered the external character of
Crosbie a good deal, but made it much more commodious inside. Here it is quite difficult to see where the seventeenth
century work ends and the nineteenth century begins: in the
drawing-room, for instance, one half of the double apartment
is old and the other new, yet there is between them a complete
harmony which unfortunately was not achieved outside. The
old oak panelling was also, where necessary, reproduced with
scrupulous fidelity—by the descendants, one might say, of the
very craftsmen who fashioned the original work.

Dr Graham's alterations include the attic dormers, one or
two windows pierced obliquely through the old walls on the
north side to give views on to the glen or the sea, the enlarging
of some of the old windows, and the addition of a new front
door. But the most striking alteration of the old house was to
heighten it—not by adding to the top of the walls but by
deepening the bottom. The house was found to be damp, and
the remedy chosen was to dig away about five feet of the earth

around the foundations—the original level of the surrounding ground can be judged from that of the lawn—and to under-build, section by section, thus providing a sort of insulation between the ground-floor and the soil. This left the original doorway in the stair-tower higher than the new ground level, and steps to lead up to it were accordingly added. The last change here was to make the original entrance into a window, so as to eliminate a draught; but the actual door, studded with iron, was left fixed in its open position. The plaster wall of the wheel-stair was also removed to reveal the old rough stone-work underneath.

The late Mrs Graham (Dr Graham's daughter-in-law) took a great pride in the house, and in the years between the World Wars it contained many rare and beautiful things: fine old furniture, Persian rugs, some carved chairs made from oak taken from the north-west door of Glasgow Cathedral which was removed during the alterations of a hundred years ago, Crown Derby china, a Botticelli triptych, and a naval dirk which once belonged to Nelson.

Mrs Graham died in 1935, and in 1946 her son sold the house and policies to the Duke of Hamilton, from whom they were acquired by the Scottish Youth Hostels Association. And thus Crosbie adds one more name—Crosbie hostel—to those of Crosbie Castle, Corsby-toure, and Crosbie-Craufurd.

6

THE KILKERRAN IMPROVERS

I

Any bias in favour of the improving lairds noticeable in this book is frankly due to my own family history, for indeed I cannot but feel impressed by the record of the improvers and their contribution to the economy of rural Scotland when I see around my own home every day the visible achievement of a typical group of them in the development of the family estate. This central part of the valley of the Water of Girvan in Carrick, mostly comprised by the northern end of Dailly parish, is in its modern aspect largely the creation of three men: my great-great-grandfather, Sir James Fergusson, fourth baronet of Kilkerran, his uncle Sir Adam Fergusson, the third baronet, and Sir Adam's father Sir James, the second baronet but better known by his judicial title of Lord Kilkerran. The work of my father, grandfather and great-grandfather, apart from the continued development of the forestry side of the estate, has chiefly been to maintain and successively modernise the structure erected on Lord Kilkerran's foundations—for he, rather than his son and grandson, was the 'improver' in the strict historical sense of the word. From the family papers of himself and his immediate successors, amplified by the evidence of the landscape itself and of maps, can be deduced the story of one estate's development: an instance typical of many in Scotland[1] but from its familiarity to me the easiest to describe.

[1] Of which the best documented is that of Monymusk, described in *Monymusk Papers* (1713–55), Scottish History Society, 1945.

THE KILKERRAN IMPROVERS

The history of Kilkerran is only one section of a considerable body of evidence refuting the assumption of textbook historians that the improvement of rural Scotland only began after the Jacobite rising of 1745 had been extinguished—as though the improvers, with some unexplained prescience, had held their hands until they were finally assured of tranquillity. There are many estates whose records prove the contrary, but such histories are often unpublished or, even when published, little read. Examples are Monymusk, where Sir Archibald Grant was building dykes, sowing grass and pease, and planting oaks and firs as early as 1719;[1] Penicuik, where Sir John Clerk the same year was 'bussied' about the plantations and nurseries on the banks of the Midlothian Esk which he had begun in 1709, and in the course of thirty years 'planted more than 300,000 trees';[2] and the many lairds whose improvements are discussed in the transactions of 'The Honourable the Society of Improvers in the Knowledge of Agriculture in Scotland', founded in 1723.

Kilkerran lies in a district which at the beginning of the eighteenth century was agriculturally as backward as the rest of Scotland but seems to have been well regarded by contemporaries. Its fertility had been praised generations before by the historian George Buchanan,[3] who spent some time in Carrick when he was tutor to Gilbert Kennedy, afterwards third Earl of Cassillis. A less friendly observer, an English spy who reported on Carrick between 1563 and 1566, but did not apparently venture more than a mile or two up the Girvan valley, dismissed it as 'a barrant cuntree but for bestiall;' adding, 'The people for the moste part spekeht Erishe.'[4]

and *Life and Labour on an Aberdeenshire Estate*, 1735–50, Third Spalding Club, 1946, both edited by Dr Henry Hamilton.

[1] *Monymusk Papers*, pp. 72–3.

[2] *Memoirs of Sir John Clerk of Penicuik*, Scottish History Society, 1892, pp. 74, 99, 136.

[3] *'Pascuis fecunda, nec infelix frumento.'—Rerum Scoticarum Historia*, ed. Robert Fribarn, 1727, p. 13.

[4] *Archaeological and Historical Collections relating to the Counties of Ayr and Wigton*, vol. iv (1884), p. 17.

But observers of the seventeenth century had commented admiringly on its 'plesant, lairge, and fruitfull wallages',[1] and 'adiacent little pretty greine hilles, intermingled with some hadder and mosse'.[2] The Rev. William Abercrummie, writing soon after 1690,[3] grew lyrical on the 'faire pleasant prospect' of the valley, whose 'many pleasant houses', the '*amoenae villae*' commended by Buchanan, stood surrounded by gardens, orchards, woods and other 'accommodations'.[4] Macky, some twenty-five years later, also noted the district as 'a beautiful little vale for some miles'.[5] All this admiration had been inspired by the Girvan valley in its unimproved state—which, we may be sure, was pretty wild.

The lands which the future Lord Kilkerran and his descendants were to take in hand were not, for the most part, the old family estate of Kilkerran, which consisted of a few hill farms near the tall stone tower where the Fergussons had lived at least since the middle of the fifteenth century and probably a good while before that. He was not, indeed, in his early childhood, in the line of succession to the property, which had descended from his great-grandfather Sir John Fergusson— that hot-blooded cavalier whose mother had been the daughter of Alexander Forrester of Garden, and who was later knighted by Charles I. In Lord Kilkerran's boyhood the laird of Kilkerran was his cousin Alexander (Sir John's grandson of the elder line), a man whom subsequent family tradition remembered as 'foolish', and who was cited for scandalous behaviour to 'compeir' before the kirk session of Dailly in 1699. Either the ordeal of Alexander's penance, from which he was not finally released for nearly a year, or the poverty to which he and his father had been reduced by the fines laid on the royalist

[1] I can find this word in no dictionary but take it to mean 'glens'.

[2] Quoted from Sir James Balfour's Collections in *The Historie of the Kennedyis*, ed. Robert Pitcairn, 1830, p. 187.

[3] When the new parish church of Dailly, which he calls 'of late erected', was built.

[4] 'A Description of Carrict' in *Macfarlane's Geographical Collections*, Scot. Hist. Soc., vol. ii, 1907, pp. 10–12.

[5] *A Journey Through Scotland*, 1723, p. 328.

CROSBIE-CRAUFURD: ORIGINAL PORTION

Photographed by the author on the day of its opening as a Youth Hostel, 1947

Sir John, determined him to leave the parish—which meant leaving Kilkerran. He had already sold a good part of the family property in 1696, and in 1701 he parted with all that remained of it—'the tower, fortalice, manors, lakes, houses, edifices, gardens, orchards, fishings,' and so forth. The purchaser of both lots was his first cousin, Mr John Fergusson of Barclanachan, advocate, the father of the future Lord Kilkerran.

Sir John Fergusson, who about 1650 had 'retired abroad till the Restauration, a short time after which he died',[1] had left, besides other children, a son named Simon or Simeon, of whom I can discover little, except that the Presbytery of Ayr included him with his father in their list of 'disaffected persons' (i.e. opposed to the Covenanters) in 1645.[2] Being a great-grandfather of Sir Adam Fergusson's, he was presumably that one at whom James Boswell, an illwisher of Sir Adam's, obscurely gibed as having been 'a messenger',[3] meaning, perhaps, a messenger-at-arms. He married Jean Craufurd, the daughter of a small laird in the neighbouring parish of Kirkoswald, Craufurd of Balsarroch, whose house Abercrummie brackets with Thrave as 'obscure countrey dwellings';[4] and he 'acquired the lands of Auchinwin and others, parts of the estate of Kilkerran, by adjudication led at his instance against his brother Alexander',[5] the father of the 'foolish' son. It may have been at Auchinwin, near Maybole, that Simon's grandson James was born in 1688.

Simon was alive in 1675, when he bought two small farms from the Earl of Cassillis, but was dead before 1686, in which

[1] Nisbet's *A System of Heraldry*, p. 411.
[2] Paterson's *History of Ayrshire* (1863 ed.): *Kyle*, p. clviii.
[3] Charles Rogers: *Boswelliana*, pp. 283–4; cp. a covert reference in *The Private Papers of James Boswell*, vol. xiii, p. 233.
[4] *Macfarlane's Geographical Collections*, vol. ii, p. 21.
[5] Playfair's *Baronetage*, Appendix, pp. lxxiv–lxxv. My grandfather noted a tradition that the account of the Fergusson family in this work was 'written or revised by Lord Hermand', Sir Adam's younger brother. Some of it at least was written by Sir Adam himself, for a draft of certain passages is among his papers.

year John Fergusson, his son, began the recovery of the family fortunes. John's mother had, under her marriage contract, a 'locality' of Auchinwin, that is to say an appropriation to her in liferent of that property, and from this she had saved 'some thousand merks'. With this sum added to the proceeds of five years at the Bar, where he had been 'eminently successful',[1] John Fergusson was able to buy an old Kennedy property called Barclanachan (earlier, Balmaclanachan) which marched with the Kilkerran lands to the north.[2] It had been bought in 1684 by James Whitefoord of Dunduff,[3] whose daughter Jean John Fergusson had married the same year.[4] No doubt, therefore, the young couple acquired it at a moderate price.

Robert Kennedy of Barclanachan, who was still alive in 1722, was the last of an old family which had held land of the Earls of Cassillis since before 1502.[5] The property which passed through the laird of Dunduff's hands to John Fergusson was mostly hill pasture, comprising the modern sheep-farms of Blair, Garleffin, Doughty and Dalwyne, besides two others which survive on the modern map only as the names of hills, Knockingalloch and Auchingairn. But on the west the high rolling expanse of coarse grass, heather and moss-hags dipped steeply down into the fertile Girvan valley; and here, half a mile from the river, stood the house of Barclanachan at the foot of curving hill-spurs whose concavity faced north-west. No description of it exists, but it was probably, like the few of its contemporary neighbours that survive, a tall L-shaped stone tower. Abercrummie only mentions it briefly as 'the house of Barclanachan with its gardens and orchards all which are surrounded by wood, all the water from this downward till near Daillie being so covered with wood that it looks lyke a forrest';[6]

[1] Playfair's *Baronetage* p. lxxv.

[2] The name is on record as 'Ballemaklunican' as early as 1361 in the Cassillis Papers.

[3] General Register of Sasines, vol. 70, No. 119.

[4] Not in 1680, as stated by Playfair.

[5] When a George Kennedy of Balmaclanachan is on record (Cassillis MSS).

[6] *Macfarlane's Geographical Collections*, vol. ii, p. 11.

and he includes it in a later passage among a list of 'mansion-houses all alongst Girvan which gives a very delightfull prospect to any who from the top of the hills, that guard the same, shall look downe upon that pleasant trough'.[1]

Some of the old house of Barclanachan may have been incorporated into that which John Fergusson erected, but his new house was thoroughly modern in character. Without, it was handsomely symmetrical: within, it was spacious, with high, well lighted rooms, simply panelled and (on the first floor) dignified by vaulted ceilings. Its appearance when first built must strongly have resembled that of Melville, designed at about the same time (1692) for the first Earl of Melville by James Smith, probably with the advice of Sir William Bruce.[2] It faced north, but that gave its main rooms a fine view across the valley, and moreover turned a protecting shoulder to the prevailing south-west winds which blew along the valley from the sea, 'coming up the bottom', as Lord Kilkerran wrote forty years later, 'as from a pipe or bellows.' It was to break the assault of these winds that John Fergusson planted in 1706 a belt of silver firs, which stand to this day, beyond the south side of the Barclanachan burn, on ground which he had got in tack in 1705 from his neighbour Alexander Kennedy of Drummellan.

The old tower of Kilkerran, whose name was transferred to the new Barclanachan, was abandoned after 1701, though time and weather needed another century and a half to bring it to ruin, and one lofty gable of it still stands. It was in 1701 that John Fergusson became the laird of Kilkerran. He had in 1696 bought a considerable parcel of the family estate, lying between Barclanachan and the old tower, from his cousin Alexander: the farms of Murestoun, Poundland, Glengie, Maldenoch and Ballibeg. Now in 1701 he acquired 'the £10 land of old extent of Kilkerran', with all the attached farms from 'Over and Nether Penbleath', above the head of the glen,

[1] *Ibid.*, p. 20.
[2] Sir John Stirling Maxwell: *Shrines and Homes of Scotland*, 1937, p. 191.

down past Gettybeg, 'with the mill of the same,' to Balcamie
near the new-built kirk of Dailly, with the holm between
whose ditches and drystane dykes Sir John Fergusson had
pastured the troop of horse he raised for Montrose.[1]

The sasine of 14 May 1701 proceeded on a charter from King
William III erecting the estate, which former Fergussons had
held of the Earls of Cassillis as superiors, into 'a free barony
called the barony of Kilkerran'. With the charter and sasine
the new laird acquired another document which established
his title even beyond its strict legality. His outgoing cousins,
as Nisbet recorded, 'Alexander the father, John and William
the two sons, sign a separate writ, which was in my hands, by
which they cheerfully renounce all interest and title they in any
manner of way pretend to the above lands, and wishes a happy
enjoyment to the said Sir John and his. Yet still'—the careful
genealogist added—'the primogeniture and right of blood, as
heir-male, is in the person of William Fergusson of Auchin-
blain, who carries the ancient arms of the family'.[2]

'The said Sir John' did not enjoy that dignity in 1701; but
it was not long delayed. He had now an eminent position at
the Scots Bar; he was a considerable landed proprietor; and,
even if lacking 'the primogeniture and right of blood', he
was the territorial representative of a family which a former
Lyon King of Arms had listed among 'the most ancient
gentrey' of Carrick.[3] Thus he had become enough of a figure
to be included among those whom Queen Anne's ministers
thought it wise to recommend for the distribution of honours
in the tense autumn of 1703 after the Scots Parliament
had passed the Act of Security;[4] and on St Andrew's Day of
that year 'Magister Joannes Fergussone de Kilcarran' was

[1] The local tradition was recorded by Sir Adam; also by his
nephew Sir James from the recollections of Lord Hermand. Cp.
Paterson's *History of Ayrshire: Kyle*, p. clix.

[2] Alexander Nisbet: *A System of Heraldry*, p. 412.

[3] Balfour's Collections quoted in *The Historie of the Kennedyis*,
p. 185.

[4] See John Struthers: *The History of Scotland from the Union to
1748*, 1827–8, vol. i, p. xiii.

created a baronet of Scotland. He matriculated a coat-of-arms in 1719.

Sir John took some part in public life in Ayrshire—he was agent for the town of Ayr in 1704[1] and was appointed a Deputy Lieutenant for the county in 1717—but I have found little record of his work as an improver. The rental-book, kept in his own hand, shows careful attention to the affairs of his estate; but it also illustrates how in his day agriculture in the valley was still primitive, even though potatoes had been grown in Dailly parish as early as 1692.[2] The rent of Murestoun, one of Sir John's best farms, as late as 1727 was only £120 Scots 'of siller rent', and the rest in kind—a stone of butter, a lamb, twelve hens and twelve chickens.

The first improvement of the estate was in afforestation; but this was not due to Sir John himself, despite the planting of the belt of silver firs in 1706 and of three groups of others in 1707—which likewise still survive, grown to enormous size—in the deep shelter of the Lady Glen. This work was taken in hand by Sir John's eldest son James, who caught the mania for improvement at the early age of twenty-three. 'I came pretty early', he writes, 'to take a liking to planting, and which my father gave me full latitude in, tho' little disposed to it himself. . . . I begun in the spring 1711 to sow for nurseries—the very year I was admitted advocat and came to live with my father in the country—and spring 1715 begun the hill planting and soon made great progress in it.' Besides planting for timber he improved the picturesque setting of the house, designing a 'great diagonal' of beeches to mount the slope of the bank behind it and clumps of others in well chosen spots around; and he considered opening up the view across the river which the natural wood 'lyke a forrest' obscured.

His letters to his newly wedded wife, Jean Maitland, grand-daughter of the fifth Earl of Lauderdale, a few months after

[1] Paterson's *History of Ayrshire: Carrick*, p. 231.
[2] Rev. George Turnbull, D.D.: *A South Ayrshire Parish*, 1908, p. 91.

their marriage, reveal the improver in his element, concerned for the moment not with agriculture but with amenity, and planning amiable little surprises for the partner to whom he was devoted but whom he had been obliged for the moment to leave with her mother and her first baby in Edinburgh. 'I am never within doors while it is fair', he writes; and, some days later, 'Our weather is so very bad that I get but very slow advances made in my projects tho' I do keep the lads pretty closs to work while they can stand out.' One letter goes into particulars on a new walk, and from their evidence its course was traced and uncovered some forty years ago; we know it to-day as 'Lady Jean's Walk'.

'I must now for your diversion (having nothing worth writing other to tell you) let you know what progress I have made in spite of the bad weather. I have made the walk I intended from the entry to the great bank up throw the old timber called the hag,[1] and pierced the view throw the park, and have when in the hag carryed off a spiral walk which leads up to [the] head of it into the great diagonal which realy looks extreamly pretty. It['s] very natural and will I'm sure please you. I have near finished the little cover I intended for the rabbets by a little roofed house added to their former habitation in which they could not subsist in the winter time, and we have agreed for the building of a pidgeon house. I hope to find the pleasure of a pidgeon pye—you know when. This progres I have made amidst very bad weather which has cost the fellows many a wet skin tho' I belive their throats were not so oft wet as they would have been had my lamb been here, as they now and then say.'

Sir John Fergusson died, aged 75, on 14 February 1729, and was buried in the abandoned tower of Kilkerran. The last addition to the estate in his lifetime, which James bought in his name in 1728, was Dalduff, two miles up the river, once the home of a cadet branch of the Kilkerran Fergussons, and des-

[1] Jamieson quotes two instances of *hag* as meaning 'one cutting or felling of a certain quantity of copse wood'; and Cockburn of Ormistoun often uses the word in this sense.

cribed by Abercrummie as 'a small stone house with ane orchard and good corne feilds about it'.[1] It was sold in 1946.

II

After Sir John's death his son continued the work of improving the estate with ardour and possibly now with more capital to finance it. One of his first cares, during the summer following his father's death, was to go carefully through the titles to various parts of the estate and get them correctly 'registrat', for Sir John 'had generally omitted to registrat his material writes', to the uneasiness of his more methodical son. Sir James made 'doubles' of all the inventories, one copy for the charter room at Kilkerran 'to be put up with the papers, and another to ly at Edinburgh'.

For a few years during the next decade it looked as if Sir James's energies might have to be directed away from the improvement of land. John, fifteenth Earl of Sutherland, Lady Jean's maternal grandfather, died in June 1733, and his grandson and successor, William, Lord Strathnaver, had to vacate the seat for the county of Sutherland which he had occupied in the House of Commons for six years. In March 1734[2] Sir James Fergusson became member for Sutherland in his place. The seat was virtually in the gift of the reigning Earl of Sutherland, being unique in that the qualified Sutherland voters were freeholders holding land not, as in other Scottish counties, of the King but of the Earl of Sutherland. It was natural that the new Lord Sutherland should choose his cousin to succeed him, for the old Earl had treated Fergusson with great friendliness and turned frequently to him for legal advice on rather delicate family matters. But Sir James was no mere tame nominee. He had high principles and a strong sense of public duty, and though he was member for Sutherland for only a few months the reputation clung to him ten

[1] *Macfarlane's Geographical Collections*, vol. ii, p. 11.
[2] According to the *Gentleman's Magazine* for that month, though the *Return of Members of Parliament* gives the date of his election as May 30.

years later of having 'by his own activity and merit got into Parliament'.[1]

It was another promotion that obliged him to retire from Westminster. He had hoped for a judge's gown since at least March of 1730, when Lord Kimmerghame died.[2] But it was not till 7 November 1735 that he was raised to the Bench in place of the deceased Lord Ormistoun and took his seat in the Court of Session as Lord Kilkerran. This automatically made him incapable of remaining in the Commons, under a clause which Sir Robert Walpole and Lord Islay (later third Duke of Argyll) had, in March 1734, inserted into a bill dealing with elections, for the sole purpose of excluding from Parliament James Erskine, Lord Grange. The clause might be, as its principal victim said, 'as ridiculous as to bring bombs and cannon to batter down a silly cottage';[3] but it was passed, and brought the whole race of Scottish political judges to an end which on the whole need not be regretted. Among its early effects was the abrupt termination, twenty months later, of Sir James Fergusson's Parliamentary career. Possibly he resented it. It might well have been some sense of filial loyalty that made his eldest son rather pointedly refuse to meet Walpole nine years later.[4]

Anyway, Lord Kilkerran now had the more time to devote to rural affairs. In 1736 he achieved an ambition of more than twenty years' standing by the purchase of Drummellan, the estate lying between the former Barclanachan and the river. Its proximity had hitherto prevented any improvement schemes to the west of the house, which stood on the very march of Drummellan. David Kennedy of Drummellan, who lived in the house of Drumburle on the far side of the Water of

[1] J. D. Humphreys: *Correspondence and Diary of Philip Doddridge, D.D.*, vol. iv, p. 285.

[2] Fergusson to Hugh, third Earl of Loudoun, 5 March 1730 (Loudoun MSS).

[3] G. W. T. Omond: *The Lord Advocates of Scotland*, 1883, vol. i, p. 345.

[4] James Fergusson: *John Fergusson* (1727–50), 1948, pp. 45–6, 48–9.

Girvan, nearly opposite Drummellan, had approached Sir James in 1731, supported by his wife's uncle, Robert Kennedy of Pinmore, with a proposal to sell 'the High and Laigh Mains'; and some months later, 'just as I was upon the wing for the winter session,' with a larger proposal. 'Drummellan was at a pinch: sell to some body he must'; and although he and his advisers drove harder and harder bargains with each successive piece of ground sold, the upshot was that by 1736 Lord Kilkerran had bought all the land down to the riverside.

'The purchase', he wrote, 'was the dearest, I doubt, was ever made in Carrick. Yet considering the conveniency of it to me, I may say necessity of it, to make the place tolerable, had I omitted the opportunity, I should never have forgiven myself. . . . I might have had it much cheaper, but . . . it continues a satisfaction to me that I had it without a grudge, on the contrary that my getting of it made the man to think himself happy when he parted with it.' As with the acquisition of Kilkerran itself, gain had been sweetened by goodwill on both sides.

This purchase had considerable results, on both the amenity and the agriculture of the estate. First, Lord Kilkerran was able to lay out a garden to the west of his house. All vestige of it has long disappeared except one ancient cherry-tree which blossoms gloriously every spring, but the grass-park covering its site is still named the Pleasure Grounds. Hitherto the prospect from Lord Kilkerran's western windows had been unsightly. 'The constant [passage] to Drummellan for horse and foot had past memory been down through the meadows summer and winter, keeping especially in winter no fixed road, which could not well be in so potchy a ground. This must have been an eye sore had it been mine.'

Further, the purchase of Drummellan stimulated Lord Kilkerran's agricultural improvements. 'But for my first purchase of the part above the highway I do not think I should ever have dream'd of inclosing my own muir, the conveniency of stone for inclosing on the march between my new purchase and Glengie having been the first thing that put it in my head.'

The enclosures on the moor above the house amounted to

some 500 acres. Lord Kilkerran experimented with 'paring, burning, and liming', using lime from a quarry on his farm of Blair, a mile up the hill above Kilkerran, to get rid of the 'hadder and mosse' characteristic of the district and establish good grass. 'I am well informed', wrote Robert Maxwell of Arkland, in the transactions of the Society of Improvers, 'that . . . the common farmers in the neighbourhood, who, until they saw what he did, and what crops he got, never so much as once fancied that such barren-like ground was a subject proper for agriculture, begin now to copy after him.'[1]

No improver could wish for a better epitaph. The heartbreak of some improvers was the difficulty of getting their tenants to forsake their traditional, laborious and unremunerative methods of husbandry. One of the earliest pamphlets published by the Society of Improvers was addressed particularly to farmers who objected to the introduction of summer fallowing 'that they are poor, and cannot forego the want of a crop, and one crop cannot be expected to make up the loss of two'.[2] At Drummond Castle the Duke of Perth, when he attempted to introduce summer fallowing and the sowing of artificial grasses, found that his tenants 'disliked everything new' and 'regarded these essays as the freak of the day, and of the same stamp with race or hunting horses'.[3] Cockburn of Ormistoun, who studied the advantage of his tenants 'equal at least to the making the estate better to those who shall come after me, and I am sure much more than any advance of the rent to myself,' complained of 'the obstinate stupidity of our people— who talk of being good countrymen but act against anything can improve it'.[4] Similarly in Mull and Morven the people were described in 1732 as 'bewitched' in their adherence to the

[1] Robert Maxwell: *Select Transactions of the Honourable the Society of Improvers*, 1743, pp. 19–20.

[2] *A Treatise concerning the Manner of Fallowing of Ground*, 1724, pp. 7–8. The anonymous author was William Macintosh of Borlum.

[3] *Scotland and Scotsmen in the Eighteenth Century*, ed. Alexander Allardyce, 1888, vol. ii, p. 226.

[4] *Letters of John Cockburn of Ormistoun to his Gardener*, Scottish History Society, 1904, pp. xxiv, 91–2.

wasteful old methods of agriculture.[1] At Monymusk Sir Archibald Grant wrote vigorous exhortation to his backward tenants: 'Such of you as are diligent misapply it and won't take advice from those who know better, nor will you follow good example when you see it has good effects, but will keep straitly to the old way. But also a great many of you are idle and trifle away a good deal of your time. . . . As to your poor living I am sorry for it, but it is your own fault. For God's sake, then, be roused by the example of others and by your own reason to pursue your true interest.'[2] At Kilkerran the first improver made at least a breach in the old conservatism. It was left to his son and successor to widen it.

Lord Kilkerran's lifetime brought also many improvements to the inside of the family home. Being a modern house, it was probably never other than dignified and cheerful, and it is hard to fit it into the squalid picture of country life in the early eighteenth century rather overdrawn by Henry Grey Graham. Still, there can have been few pictures on its walls in Sir John's time, when 'artists had scanty encouragement from gentlemen who were too poor to pay for pictures and too uncivilised to care for them';[3] and there were so few books in the house that during his years as an advocate Lord Kilkerran had occasionally borrowed from the well-filled shelves of the minister of Kirkmichael, Mr James Lawrie.[4]

Lady Jean, however, having been an only child, brought some quite good portraits of her Lauderdale and Sutherland relations into the family; and a few years before his death Lord Kilkerran had himself and two of his daughers, Jean and Peggy, admirably painted by Ramsay. The girls' portraits are signed and dated 1752, so that if the judge's portrait in his robes as a Lord of Justiciary belongs to the same year it

[1] [Eighth] Duke of Argyll: *Scotland as It Was and as It Is*, second ed., 1887, pp. 255–6.
[2] *Monymusk Papers*, 1713–55, p. lxx.
[3] H. G. Graham: *The Social Life of Scotland in the Eighteenth Century*, 1928 ed., p. 68.
[4] H. G. Graham: *Literary and Historical Essays*, 1908, p. 156.

shows him as he was when he took his probably uneasy seat beside the Duke of Argyll on the bench at Inveraray for the Appin murder trial. It is much to be regretted that Lady Jean did not sit to Ramsay too—probably because two portraits of her, neither of much merit, hung in the house already.

Lord Kilkerran also began the formation of a library, later to be notably enlarged by his son Adam. As might be expected of 'one of the ablest lawyers of his time',[1] he collected many volumes on law; but others on history, theology and agriculture—among the last a handsome copy of the 1706 edition of John Evelyn's *Silva*—also bear his bookplate with the beautifully engraved coat-of-arms closely modelled on the design of that in Nisbet's *System of Heraldry*.

Of the furniture of his time little has survived in the house except a set of embroidered chairs bearing the initials of Lady Jean and three of her daughters, who worked their now faded but still graceful flowers.

Though writing of Lord Kilkerran mainly as an improver, I must spend a little space on his personal character, of whose 'probity and integrity' the tradition lingered long.[2] The family correspondence, some of which I have published elsewhere, shows an unusually affectionate and intimate family circle, whose children address their father not with the formal 'Honoured Sir' of the period but as 'Dear Pappa'. Among the earlier letters are a few from 'the old folks', Sir John and his lady, proud and happy in their successful son, their 'dear daughter' his wife, and their 'litil comrade' the eldest grandson. A generation later Lord Kilkerran appears both as an earnest and as an indulgent father, adjuring one son to make the best use of his years of study, lest he 'return . . . a mere country squire',[3] and trusting another with absolute freedom of responsibility in both route and expenditure when making the grand tour.[4]

---

[1] A. F. Tytler: *Life of Lord Kames*, vol. i, p. 36.
[2] *Ibid.*   [3] *John Fergusson, 1727–50*, p. 59.
[4] James Fergusson: *Letters of George Dempster to Sir Adam Fergusson (1756–1813)*, 1934, pp. 18, 23.

Outside the family, too, he seems to have been a congenial companion. Lord Auchinleck 'met with Lord Kilkerran and Baron Maule in a club' one summer evening in Edinburgh, and a year later spent some jolly hours with the same companions in 'the Duke's new inn' at Inveraray, where the wine was 'excellent' and Lord Kilkerran (then in his 68th year) 'drunk several bumpers in high spirits and tho' I remonstrated to him privatly against his doing it woud not refrain, and to this I impute a threatning of the gout which prevented his going to the Court at Glasgow and made him leave me the second day of the circuit'.[1] John Maule of Inverkeilor, one of the Barons of the Court of Exchequer, would have been a kindred spirit very likely to move Kilkerran to conviviality, for he was as enthusiastic a tree-planter in Angus as the other in Ayrshire.[2]

The gout Lord Kilkerran owed to such occasions so tormented his hands and feet that he had sometimes to dictate his letters and throughout his judicial career could not walk further than the garden he had made before his house. But his brain was active to the end of his life, and his kindliness extended far beyond his family circle. The second son of the harassed minister of Kirkmichael owed to Lord Kilkerran's patronage[3] the bursary that launched him on a successful career; and a tattered notebook once belonging to the tenant of one of the outlying Kilkerran farms testifies that he was a lenient landlord.

III

Lord Kilkerran died at his little house just outside Edinburgh on 20 January 1759, and his death was notable news as far away as Kelso.[4] The heir to the estate and baronetcy of Kilkerran was his second son Adam, John the eldest, an amiable

---

[1] Lord Auchinleck to John, fourth Earl of Loudoun, 29 June 1754 and 26 September 1755 (Loudoun MSS).

[2] *Registrum de Panmure*, vol. i, p. lxxxvi.

[3] National Library of Scotland MS 2968 (Culloden MSS), f. 126.

[4] *Diary of George Ridpath*, Scottish History Society, 1922, p. 226.

and promising young soldier, having died of a tuberculous complaint in 1750.

Sir Adam, whose education at Edinburgh University had been enlarged by nearly three years of continental travel, spent his early years at the Scots Bar and his prime in Parliament as member for Ayrshire. A diligent, honourable, cultivated and kindly man, he was unshakably orthodox in all that he did, and might stand as the regular type of all conscientious Lowland lairds of the middle and late eighteenth century. He did his sober duty to his county and his country, farmed and planted assiduously, lent his countenance and aid to innumerable beneficent projects, and enriched Kilkerran with many pictures and books in the best taste of his time, if not always such as posterity might wish him to have chosen. Methodical in everything, he preserved most letters that he received, and generally a 'scroll' of his answer to each. The impression left by every record of his long and well spent life is one of invincible correctitude.

At a time when 'swearing was thought the right, and the mark, of a gentleman',[1] Sir Adam was sufficiently remarkable for his restraint of language to earn from Burns the epithet of 'aith-detesting'.[2] An old woman who as a child had once seen Sir Adam in a temper described to my father how 'Sir Adam cam out and he chappit on the grund wi' his stick, and says he, "Dinna think that because I'm no swearin I'm no angry." '

Not a single sentence in Sir Adam's voluminous correspondence suggests that he ever made a joke in his life; but another anecdote preserved by local tradition hints at a dry humour on occasions. Calling for the first time on his new tenant of the farm of Whitehill, Sir Adam asked abruptly of the woman who opened the door, 'Is Cooper in?'

'*Mr* Cooper', replied the goodwife to the stranger in a reproving tone, 'is no at hame.'

[1] Lord Cockburn: *Memorials of His Time*, 1856, p. 32.
[2] *The Author's Earnest Cry and Prayer to . . . the Scotch Representatives in the House of Commons.*

'Weel,' said Sir Adam mildly, 'tell him Adam Fergusson was speirin for him'—and turned on his heel.

Serious or not, he was certainly an amiable personage. His early correspondence and account-book, during the grand tour which he began with George Dempster, his lifelong friend, and just after it, show that he led a reasonably gay social life, was well read, had good taste and judgment, and was by no means narrow-minded. An effusive young lady who was a guest at Kilkerran soon after he returned from his grand tour has preserved a partial but engaging picture of him, noted one October Sunday when bad weather had prevented the house-party from going to church at Dailly. She had formed one of the family circle 'all seated with decency and composure hearing a sermon read by so noble a youth as the eldest son of Lord K——'. She described Adam as 'genteel in his person, easie in his address, totally void of foppery or affectation, idolized by his parents, admired by everybody that know him', an attentive son and affectionate brother, 'sensible and sedate yet so chearful, upon occasions even gay, having seen so much yet never seeking opportunities of discovering his knowledge, acknowledged a fine scholar without the least tincture of pedantry'—and a great deal more to the same effect, the whole suggesting a kind of Sir Charles Grandison, for the diarist was very evidently a devoted reader of Richardson.[1]

Evidently Adam at 25 was well fitted to ensnare a young lady's heart. But he was anything but romantic himself, and can never have been frivolous. Maturity certainly sobered him still more; and 'enthusiasm', that bugbear of the orthodox Georgian, was abhorrent to him. Between him and the volatile James Boswell there was a natural and unconquerable antipathy, despite their early acquaintance and the long friendship of their fathers. The dislike for him recorded several times in James Boswell's journals and occasional writings seems to

[1] Diary of Peggy Hope, afterwards Mrs Thomas Thomson, from a transcript by Dr Thomas Lauder Thomson (MS in the possession of Mr George Burnett, Old Parsonage, Calderbridge, Cumberland, to whom I am indebted for permission to quote it).

have been fixed by Sir Adam's evasion of a subscription-list for Corsican relief which 'Corsica Boswell' was pressing on his acquaintance in 1769[1]; but Boswell's violent zeal for the Douglas side in the great Douglas Cause had already estranged him from the advocate who had prepared the Hamilton 'memorial'. Jealousy of Sir Adam's long tenure of the Ayrshire seat in Parliament was certainly an ingredient, and appears very strongly in a venomous letter on Ayrshire politics which Boswell contributed to the *Public Advertiser* of 27 July 1785, in which he observed that it was 'very disagreeable . . . to be obliged to descend from recording the wisdom and wit of Dr JOHNSON, to a contest about *Sir Adam Fergusson*'.[2]

Not that Sir Adam could not like and be liked by those of far different temperament to his own. 'You never appear to me more amiable,' wrote the versatile and speculative George Dempster, 'than when I see your grave face and sound head prepared to blow all my speculations into the air from whence they came'.[3] Sir Adam's interests were wide. In his young days he had even been one of the group of Edinburgh gentlemen who subscribed to send James Macpherson into the Highlands in search of the presumed 'epic' that afterwards appeared as 'Fingal'[4] and more than a quarter of a century later he took the trouble to collect an old Gaelic poem himself in Skye.[5] In 1768 he was chosen Lord Rector of Glasgow University in opposition to Adam Smith.[6] His friends included men of such

[1] *Ex inform.* Professor Frederick A. Pottle.

[2] I owe the discovery of this letter to Dr L. W. Sharp, the librarian of the University of Edinburgh. It is not recorded in Professor Pottle's *The Literary Career of James Boswell*.

[3] *Letters of George Dempster to Sir Adam Fergusson*, p. 172.

[4] It was not, as often stated, his better known contemporary Dr Adam Ferguson, the philosopher, who was in this group. See Dr Hugh Blair's letter to Henry Mackenzie, 20 December 1797, in the *Report of the Committee of the Highland Society on the Authenticity of the Poems of Ossian*, 1805, Appendix, p. 58.

[5] See my article 'An Erse Poem' in *An Gaidheal* for February and March, 1938.

[6] James Coutts: *A History of the University of Glasgow*, 1909, p. 335.

KILKERRAN ON A SUMMER MORNING

Seen from Lord Kilkerran's 'Great Diagonal'. To the right, original block; left, 1814 addition

widely various distinction as his brother-in-law the learned
Lord Hailes, William Nairne (later Lord Dunsinnan), the dull
but diligent Sir John Sinclair of Ulbster, and 'Fish' Craufurd.
Among his Ayrshire neighbours, the only one between whom
and Sir Adam there was a coldness seems to have been David,
tenth Earl of Cassillis, who owned a good deal of the land
across the river from Kilkerran.

Their hostility was originally political, for Sir Adam won
the Ayrshire seat in Parliament in 1774 as the candidate of
a group of independent gentlemen against the combined
interest of three powerful peers, Cassillis, Eglinton and
Loudoun. David Kennedy of Newark, the sitting member,
was their candidate[1]: the brother of the ninth Earl of
Cassillis, whom he succeeded the following year. Sir Adam's
success was unexpected. It 'vexed' Boswell enough to
make him lose some sleep.[2] To Kennedy it may well have
been much more irritating. He had further ground for an-
noyance when he succeeded not only to his brother's title
and estates, and to the task of rebuilding Culzean to the
new and splendid designs of Robert Adam, but also to an
unfortunate dispute upon which a mass of Sir Adam's papers,
docketed with references to 'the coal cause', dwells in wearisome detail.

On the long hill forming the north-west side of the Girvan
valley, a former Earl of Cassillis had acquired the lands once
owned by the monks of Crossraguel Abbey, which included
some coal workings.[3] By 1775 Sir Adam also owned property
along the slope of the hill and had planted trees there to the
extent of 'near an hundred acres'. The coal under the surface
remained, however, Cassillis property, and the workings, on
what was still Cassillis ground, were let to a tacksman named

[1] *Scottish Historical Review*, vol. xxvi, pp. 128–30.
[2] *The Private Papers of James Boswell*, vol. x, p. 29.
[3] The 'coalheugh of Yellowlee' is mentioned in the Cassillis MSS
in a charter of 1566. But according to the Rev. C. H. Dick (*Highways and Byways in Galloway and Carrick*, 1916, p. 385) 'there is
evidence of coal having been wrought in this district so long ago
as 1415'.

Cumming. In 1749[1] part of the workings had caught fire, and they continued to burn intermittently underground for many years. Expert opinion considered a closure of the workings the best if not the only way to smother the fire, and Sir Adam employed men to fill up the old Dalzellowlie pit on his ground, and planted the blackened slopes above it, 'labouring many years', as he said, 'to convert a nusance and a deformity into a beauty'.

Cumming, however, rashly continued to work the coal on Lord Cassillis's ground. He 'was in desperate circumstances and probably did not care what mischief he did, provided he made a little profit to himself'. He pushed his operations up to and under the march, and in the autumn of 1775 the fire broke out once more on the surface and destroyed four or five acres of Sir Adam's planting. Sir Adam took legal action to stop him. 'To my surprise', he wrote, 'the matter was taken up in the name of Lord Cassillis, and the bill of suspension was opposed for his Lordship by his counsel and agents.'

At this point Sir Adam happened to depart to spend the winter in Bath, and on 30 November, Thomas, ninth Earl of Cassillis, died. But the machine of the law ground its unrelenting way onward, and its unsympathetic progress provided the not unnatural cause of the new Earl's grievance. A long and bitter sentence in a letter he wrote to Sir Adam on 8 January 1776 explains it:

'Was it kind or like a neighbour to send a messenger with four or five attendants to my brother's house when his disease was hasting fast to the fatal period to which it came, and to send again the same disagreeable objects a few days before his death, and as if intended to make my misery more compleat to rouse me from that melancholy I was so justly under, with a summons against myself upon the morning of the day immediatly after my brother's interment?'

[1] The date is given categorically by Mr Dick (*op. cit.*, p. 386) but may be only derived from the phrase 'about 45 years ago' in the *Statistical Account of Scotland* (Kirkoswald), vol. x, p. 497, published in 1794.

Sir Adam apologised for this unfeeling procedure for which he had not been responsible, but stuck to his resolve to have his trees protected. His determination was not unreasonable. By the summer of 1777 the fire had 'most sensibly advanced towards Tradonnock' so that there was 'no passing that way for smoke'. 'The coal cause' dragged on for nearly two years. The fire smouldered yet in Lord Cassillis's memory in 1779[1]; and in the hill itself it burned long after both he and Sir Adam were in their graves, still emitting spasmodic smoke and gas within living memory. To this day, although the fire has long been extinguished, and coal is no more worked on the scene of the quarrel, the name of 'the Burning Hill' persists.

Sir Adam continued his planting. By the time he retired from Parliament in 1796, had his portrait nobly painted by Raeburn, and settled down for his old age, still a bachelor, with his eldest sister Jean to keep house for him, he had transformed the valley with 'about 400 Scots acres' of trees.[2] By the end of the century he had bridged the river at Drumgirnan ford, and carried a new road from it up on to the Burning Hill to join the old road to Maybole, running along its lower slopes above the valley which was now all reclaimed from the swamps and thickets of a hundred years earlier. In his old age he could look round upon his work and call it good.

He could have desired, for he could conceive, no better heritage than Kilkerran. 'I am convinced', he wrote, 'that there is not a climate to be found superior to this here, taking the whole year round (I wish, however, I could be relieved of the spring).' And again, one January, 'My opinion, founded on long experience, most certainly is, that there is not probably a milder air in the winter months than that in which I now sit'— in Great Britain, he meant, for he was discounting the claims of Devon. If the south-westerly gales sometimes brought down an old tree or two, Sir Adam did not complain. 'I believe', he

[1] *The Private Papers of James Boswell*, vol. xiii, p. 233.
[2] *Statistical Account of Scotland* (Dailly), vol. x, p. 43. The Scots acre is 6150·4 sq. yds. as opposed to the English acre of 4840 sq. yds. '400 Scots acres' is therefore over 508 English acres.

observed, 'upon a moderate computation, for every one blown down, I plant 5000.'

From the windows of Kilkerran, or as he rode to church at Dailly, where his old friend Mr Thomas Thomson the minister[1] had 'corn and clover fields in excellent order, and hedges growing vigorously',[2] Sir Adam could survey the improvements of his earlier years. Unlike his father, he had begun not with planting the hills but with reclaiming the bottom of the valley, whose fertile soil had in his youth been still covered with 'natural woods of oak and birch'.[3] He has left a valuable account of these operations in a letter to Andrew Wight,[4] who surveyed and reported on the improvements in many parts of Scotland in the late 1770's, but failed to find Sir Adam at home when he visited Kilkerran. The district struck Wight, when he entered it up the road from the south, as 'a narrow, but pleasant valley, of a good soil. . . . There,' he wrote, 'in different fields, I saw various operations of husbandry carried on with industry and attention. The inclosures in perfection, both hedges and stone walls. Lime is the only manure used. I saw a number of sheep in a large inclosure opposite to the house, of different kinds, Dorchester, Cully, Bakewell, and also the breed of the country'—presumably blackface. Wight described 'the progress of agriculture in that part of the country' as 'chiefly owing to Sir Adam himself', thus echoing the tribute paid to Lord Kilkerran by Maxwell of Arkland thirty-five years before.

In his letter to Wight, Sir Adam recalled his memory of the countryside 'when there was scarce an inclosure in it but some few round the gentlemen's seats, when there was not a pound of grass seed sown from one end of it to the other, and when the

[1] The father (by his second wife) of two remarkable sons, Thomas Thomson the antiquary and John Thomson ('of Duddingston') the landscape painter, both of whom were born in the manse of Dailly.

[2] Andrew Wight: *Recent State of Husbandry in Scotland*, 1778, vol. iii, p. 156.

[3] Colonel Fullarton's *Report on Ayrshire* to the Board of Agriculture, 1793, pp. 41-2.

[4] Wight, *op. cit.*, pp. 157-64.

whole attention of the farmer, and the whole dung of the farm, was applied to a few acres, while the rest was totally neglected.

'With regard to myself,' continued Sir Adam, 'my object has been to turn the farms in my own possession into good grass as soon as possible.' He described how he had blasted the erratic boulders in the holms with gunpowder, cleared the fields 'of shrubs and bushes', drained them, limed them at the rate of 'an hundred bolls to the Scots acre', and introduced a proper rotation of crops. Despite the Dorchester and Bakewell flocks, he professed himself dubious of the prospects of 'the English sheep in our hills'. He believed in the native breeds of both sheep and cattle. 'The utmost length that I think it would be safe to go, would be to endeavour to raise our own breed by a mixture with the English; and even that should be done with great caution'.

Regarding his tenants, Sir Adam was somewhat sparing of his praises. But he conceded that several deserved commendation 'for their attention and industry', and that there was 'a remarkable alteration to the better, both in their knowledge and management, since I began to attend to country affairs'. They were now all keen on proper enclosures, were 'getting into the practice, more or less, of sowing grass seeds', and, above all, 'the distinction of croft and field land, except among some of the poorest sort, is, in a manner, entirely abolished'.

This last was a notable step forward. Only fourteen years before, a Scottish agricultural writer had described the old system of infield and outfield in terms suggesting that it was still normal.[1] At Kilkerran Sir Adam's progressive measures had already relegated it to the past, partly by taking as some of his tenants 'farmers of great skill in husbandry' and partly by giving all his tenants long leases binding them to modern methods of manuring and cropping.[2] By 1794 the result of his and his father's policy had contributed to increase the valued rent of Dailly parish to more than three times that of thirty

[1] *A Treatise of Agriculture*, 1762, p. 101, note. The anonymous author was Adam Dickson.

[2] *Statistical Account of Scotland* (Kirkoswald), vol. x, p. 487.

years earlier, and farm servants' wages, over sixty years, from six to nine times. 'The rising wages of common labour and domestic service', observed Mr Thomson in drawing up the 'Statistical Account' of the parish, 'ought, by an indifferent spectator, to be regarded as one of the happiest effects of increasing industry and opulence.'[1] In another part of Ayrshire another minister remarked that despite the steady rise in wages the price of oatmeal, 'the chief article of living, is nearly, at an average, the same it was 20 or 30 years ago.'[2]

For many years Sir Adam wrote regularly to his nephew and destined heir, James Fergusson, who after some years in India as a junior partner in the firm of Fergusson and Fairlie of Calcutta returned to Scotland in 1799 with the recommendation of one of his seniors that 'a nobler young man is not within my acquaintance'. A few months after his return James married his cousin Jean, the second daughter of Sir David Dalrymple, Lord Hailes, who had married one of Sir Adam's sisters. The same year he joined the Ayrshire and Renfrewshire Militia, who were employed in coastal defence in various parts of England during the period when Napoleon threatened invasion. James had risen to command them by 1807, but retired in June, his health being uncertain, and took a house in Essex, Thoby Priory; he lived there till 1810, when he settled in George's Square, Edinburgh. His first wife died after less than four years of marriage, and in December 1804 he married Henrietta Duncan, daughter of the admiral who was the victor of Camperdown. His first wife bore him three children, and his second thirteen.

Sir Adam's rather long-winded letters to his nephew contain much good advice, a few reflections on current political and military affairs, occasional reminiscences of his own career, and numerous details about the affairs of Kilkerran estate. He shows an avuncular interest in James's large family and sometimes offers tentative and tactful advice concerning their health or education. His last extant letter, written when he

[1] *Statistical Account of Scotland* (Dailly), pp. 43–4, 51, note.
[2] *Ibid.* (Kilmaurs), vol. ix, p. 357.

was over eighty, embraces some reflections on the distant past, the present and the future of Kilkerran, yet barely allows any glimpse into the inner mind of the undemonstrative man who had been so careful a steward of the heritage he had administered for over half a century. Age had not diminished his shrewdness or his realism.

He recommended James to try to acquire the remainder of the Burning Hill from Lord Cassillis—this was the twelfth Earl, afterwards first Marquess of Ailsa. The fire in the hill still persisted. 'That his Lordship will attempt working the coal in its present state and while the fire lasts, I think impossible. . . . That there are two seams of coal in the upper part of the hill which the fire has not touched I have good reason to believe.[1] These cannot be wrought while the fire continues: but when it is extinguished, which it must be in time, there will be nothing to hinder these two seams from being wrought; in other words the whole planting up as far as the nursery being destroyed. It is to that event that I look forward; and as it is for the family and for posterity that I am acting, I cannot but consider the acquisition of the coal, though of little consequence in the present circumstances, to be more material for the future prospect.'

There was also 'the little possession of the Ruglen', an island of Cassillis property on the lower slope of the hill some distance below the coal workings, which Sir Adam felt should be acquired, and one or two other farms of which he had not gained complete possession. 'My grandfather', he told James, 'purchased the superiority of part of his estate from the curators of John [eighth] Earl of Cassillis[2] at the beginning of the last century. He would have got the whole for the asking, as the affairs of that family were then embarrassed; but mist the

[1] But he had told Henry Dundas in 1777, during 'the coal cause' against the tenth Lord Cassillis, that 'of the three places of the hill in question, in one there is no coal of any value to work; in another it is impossible to subsist for heat; and in the third, I think, there is not above one acre of coal . . . a matter certainly of very small value'.

[2] Born 1700, served heir to his father 1704, and died 1759.

opportunity. This my father has often regretted to me; but said that he had always abstained from speaking about it to his father, as he saw that he reproached himself with the neglect. This, I own, has always given me a strong desire to have these superiorities. . . . The acquisition . . . would make me the immediate vassal of the crown in the whole estate, with the exception of one farm, Tradonnock, which holds of Sir Hew Hamilton, and which therefore you would have little difficulty to acquire.'[1] Sir Adam suggested that Lord Cassillis might be persuaded to exchange Ruglen for 'a slip of land' owned by Kilkerran on the north side of Mochrum Hill in Kirkoswald parish, 'quite out of sight from every quarter but from the leading entry to Culzean. . . . But,' the old man concluded, 'as my personal concern in the matter is very small, I should not wish to enter into any transaction, without your concurrence, in which you have so much more concern than myself.'

Though occasionally troubled by the gout, but to nothing like the same extent as his father, Sir Adam was still active enough at seventy-nine to go on a visit to Ulster with some of his nieces who wanted to see the Giant's Causeway. His last years must have had their lonely moments, for all his contemporaries in the family were now dead except his brother Lord Hermand. But the Fergusson and Dalrymple nieces often visited him at Kilkerran, and James's sister Kitty settled down there to look after her uncle in the summer of 1812.

He was very ill that winter, and did not live to see another. During his last illness in September 1813, his servant Primrose, according to family tradition, fetched his drinking-water every day from his favourite spring. He died early in the morn-

[1] Sir Hew Dalrymple, fourth baronet of North Berwick, took the name and arms of Hamilton on succeeding his uncle in the estate of Bargany, which marched with Kilkerran. This was his son, Sir Hew Dalrymple Hamilton (1774–1834), who had been M.P. for Ayrshire 1803–6. He and James Fergusson had married sisters (daughters of Admiral Duncan), so that there would be 'little difficulty' in getting this concession from one who was both a neighbour and a near connection.

ing of the 25th, James, who had been summoned by express, arriving just too late to see him. 'We have few such men among us,' wrote Robert Jamieson the antiquary some months later, adding that Sir Adam 'almost seemed to belong to another age, and another state of society, more perfect than that we live in';[1] and the *Scots Magazine* published a warm eulogy of 'this venerable and respectable baronet'.[2]

IV

Sir James Fergusson, who succeeded his uncle at the age of 38, added one more chapter to the Kilkerran improvements, but he acted much more impulsively and in some respects less prudently than his uncle and grandfather. The inheritance of a large and by now very prosperous estate seems to have gone somewhat to his head, which was little more business-like than that of his father Charles, who had died in 1804, and whose financial misadventures had caused Sir Adam a good deal of worry. At all events, finding his income some five times what it had formerly been, Sir James embarked almost at once on extensive operations which were far beyond his means. Sir Adam had never spent more than £2,000 a year, including not only his household and personal expenses but also 'the large sum which keeping up and improving this place requires'. Sir James poured out his income and drew on his credit with such carefree enthusiasm that two years after his succession he found himself deep in debt to the tune of £70,000.

'I own I did not anticipate it', wrote his uncle Lord Hermand, to whom he applied for advice. 'Still, I do not wish to look back, though I must own there is something mysterious about the whole business.' His advice was to the point. Sir James must satisfy his creditors by putting himself into the hands of trustees, establish a sinking fund to pay off his debts, and live on fifteen hundred a year till they were discharged. 'This residue may appear small, and certainly is not adequate to a great establishment of servants, and other articles of

[1] *Letters of George Dempster to Sir Adam Fergusson*, p. 394.
[2] *Scots Magazine*, vol. lxxv, p. 879.

luxury. Neither will it afford the erection of buildings and gardens, extremely proper in an estate of £10,000 a year, but nowise suited to present circumstances.' But this residue, added the judge with characteristic directness, would allow Sir James 'to bring up his numerous family as other families just as good have been brought up'. The probable alternative was for the creditors to arrest the rents of the estate, or the owner's liferent of it—'and how he is to support his family in the mean time, I cannot form even a conjecture'.

Sir James, presumably, had to agree, for his affairs were somehow straightened out a good while before his death in 1838; but an endorsement of his on one of Lord Hermand's later letters suggests that he grumbled at first a good deal at the discipline which he was obliged to undergo.

The changes brought about by his expenditure were certainly considerable. He enlarged the house, employing the stones of the ruined tower of Drummellan,[1] and built two round-ended wings on to its western face, to which he transferred the main entrance. One wing contained a handsome drawing-room and a vast kitchen below it. In the opposite one were two large nurseries to house the growing tribe of young Fergussons. Sir James also threw the old garden to the west of the house into grass and laid out a new walled garden of some five acres half a mile away to the north. In the new fashion, he enclosed his policies, and in the old he continued to plant woods. But outside the private grounds he, too, made his contribution to the improvement of the valley and the progress of Ayrshire farming.

Less than a month after Sir Adam's death Sir James was writing of his plans to lay out a new road up the valley towards Maybole in co-operation with three neighbouring lairds, Sir Hew Hamilton of Bargany, Quintin Kennedy of Drummellan (from whose grandfather Lord Kilkerran had bought most of the Drummellan lands), and James Fergusson of Crosshill, Principal Clerk of Session.[2] The last of these was an enthusi-

[1] Paterson's *History of Ayrshire* (Carrick), p. 210.
[2] He was no relation to the Kilkerran family.

astic improver who fifteen years before had helped Sir Adam
Fergusson and Thomas Kennedy of Dunure to plan the road
from Maybole to the Garpin bridge over the Water of Girvan.[1]
The projected new road was to join up with it at the Garpin
bridge—where the modern village of Crosshill was built some
years later—'keeping generally the opposite side of the river
from the present road and which now intended line will be
mostly quite flat instead of going over the top of every hill as
at present.' Besides the promoters, 'the public', Sir James
added, 'will also be materially benefited.' The claim was well
justified, since the project resulted in what is to-day the main
public road up the valley from opposite Kilkerran to Crosshill.
Sir James contributed to his share of the road a handsome
stone bridge where it crossed the river, which was completed
in 1825 and named Hamilton Bridge in compliment to his
friend Sir Hew.

This performance, like some others, may be set to Sir James's
credit against his early extravagances, in reference to which
old George Dempster wrote banteringly to him on 28 December 1813, while Sir James and his wife were spending a gay
winter in Edinburgh, 'I assume some authority over Lady
Fergusson, and must restrict her ladyship to *one* dinner, *three*
routs, and *two* balls, and *one* supper in the 24 hours. It would
be a proof of insanity, if a K.B. and his lady did not run stark,
staring mad, for six weeks every winter.'

Before Sir James was brought up short by his debts he must
at least have begun many other schemes. Some were abortive,
like his attempt, against the advice Sir Adam had given him,
to resume working the coal in the Burning Hill. He tried to
extinguish the still stubborn fire underground by flooding it.
'The plan,' observed Lord Hermand in a letter of 1 November
1814, 'was I believe formerly tried, but failed from the number
of fissures in the half calcined wastes. I fear you may have the
same obstacle to encounter.'

[1] James Fergusson of Crosshill to Thomas Kennedy of Dunure,
15 November 1798 (Dunure MSS, in the possession of Lt.-Col. J. K.
MacFarlan of Dunure).

A much more successful undertaking, which has proved highly beneficial to farming in the parish, was another joint operation between Sir James and Thomas Francis Kennedy of Dunure, and consisted of the straightening and embanking of the river's course between Sir Adam's bridge at Drumgirnan and Kennedy's house of Dalquharran, near the village of Dailly. Hitherto the river had coiled and meandered between the holms, cutting its corners at every spate and leaving the meadows waterlogged for half the summer. To-day sleek Ayrshire cows graze or fields of golden oats ripple in the breeze where once lay stagnant pools, and only in seasons of heavy rain does the water fill the curved depressions to indicate the windings of the old bed. Sir James had suggested 'laying back the banks' to Sir Adam in 1810, when Sir Adam replied that he himself had 'revolved it' in his mind, adding, 'The objection does not lye so much in the expence as in not knowing what could be done with so prodigious a quantity of earth as would have to be disposed of, and which cannot be carried to a distance.'

Tile-draining had been introduced into the parish by Mr Kennedy at Dalquharran, 'a most important improvement,' and Sir James adopted it, too, during the last years of his life. Once again the example of the laird led the way in an agricultural reform, for after Sir James had begun tile-draining in his own fields he was 'followed in it by one of his principal tenants'.[1]

With the curbing of the Girvan's waters, the last major improvement to the estate was completed. Sir James helped to found the still flourishing Ayrshire Agricultural Society in 1835, and died three years afterwards, leaving Kilkerran to the less grandiose but more prudent management of his eldest son Charles, of whose wedding-day in 1829, which Sir James attended in a red coat, there is a glimpse in the pages of Lord Cockburn.[2] Sir Charles added to the estate in 1845 the small property of Drumburle, across the river, the last fragment of the former Drummellan lands.

But for the appearance of the railway, which came down

[1] *New Statistical Account of Scotland* (Dailly), vol. v, p. 387.
[2] *Letters on the Affairs of Scotland*, 1874, p. 220.

from Ayr twenty years later, the absorption of some small holdings on the hillsides into larger farms, and the slow waxing and waning of subsequent generations of trees, the main appearance of the valley has altered little since Sir James's death 110 years ago. It still breaks upon the traveller's eye, as he comes southward from Maybole, green and fertile, 'gashed with glens and patched with plantations,' as pleasantly as, in Sir James's day, it broke upon the sentimental regard of the poet Hew Ainslie.[1] The age of the improvers was ended, and other men entered into their labours. The traveller who passes down Sir James's road, and looks across Sir Adam's fields at the silver-grey house set against the dark masses of his and Lord Kilkerran's woods, may well reflect that nowhere have utility and beauty been more charmingly blended.

Ille terrarum mihi praeter omnes
Angulus ridet.

Though what I have written here concerns only those who may be called the strategists of the new agriculture and silviculture, I do not forget those whose actual labours pushed on their experiments and brought their designs to fulfilment: factors, grieves, farmers, masons, joiners, hinds, foresters and labourers of all kinds. But these belong to the great army 'which have no memorial'—save their own anonymous achievements. They left no diaries nor letters, and so as historical figures survive only by allusions and an occasional scrap of holograph writing.

We know the names of many. There was John Henry, Sir Adam's factor, who lived at Ladyburn (where I spent much of my childhood) and whose signature is almost as familiar to me as that of his employer—whom Henry served not only as factor but also as an obedient 'parchment baron' on the roll of Ayrshire voters. There was William Jackson, Sir Adam's tenant of Moorston, whose fields had 'every appearance of good husbandry, regularly conducted'.[2] There was James

[1] Hew Ainslie: *A Pilgrimage to the Land of Burns*, 1892 ed., p. 98.
[2] Wight, *op. cit.*, vol. iii, p. 156.

McMillan the ploughman Sir Adam employed, who in the late summer of 1775 'fell into a lingering distemper, which unfitted him for work, for very near two years—in all which time', John Henry recorded, 'he was maintained in the familly, having bed, board, and washing as usual' besides his full wages, and 'began to work in the year 1777, in harvest time, and has been very well ever since'. And there was 'old James Paterson at Crosshill', who, as my great-grandfather noted in his diary on 13 October 1842, was 'altogether making a beautiful job' of building 'the excellent dyke' at the head of the Lady Glen.

Coming down to the present century, there was, in my own childhood, Mungo McInnes, drainer since my grandfather's days, who knew every culvert and underground watercourse on the estate as a surgeon knows the sinews and nerves of the human body; and there is to-day David Andrew, estate joiner like his father before him, whose craftsmanship has contributed something to the fabric of almost every building on the property. One conspicuous monument of David's skill is a gate which, nearly thirty years ago, took a first prize at the Highland Show.

Many, many others since 'the lads' who worked on Lord Kilkerran's first improvements have suffered 'many a wet skin' in the draining and fencing, the planting and building, and lie now in the kirkyards of Dailly or Crosshill. If their names are lost, their work remains, in the enduring characters of dyke and wood, field and fence, written large across the landscape of to-day.

7

INTERLUDE—AN EDINBURGH 'DOER': JAMES NASMYTH

In the background of every eighteenth-century Scottish family of standing and property was the figure of the 'doer', the lawyer who looked after the laird's business affairs in Edinburgh. To us to-day he is usually a dim figure, indicated only by the signature at the end of some dry-looking documents which turn up in the drawers or cabinets of old country houses. He did not as a rule leave behind him the kind of letters which one reads through in search of sidelights on national or social history; and the examination of his remains is a task for specialists who can understand tailzies and wadsets and the other mysteries of old Scots law.

Yet the 'doer' himself was a human being. When Robert Louis Stevenson wrote *Kidnapped*, he portrayed a lively and lovable man in the pleasant figure of Mr Rankeillour, with his Latin tags and his convenient propensity to forget his spectacles. A man who might have been Rankeillour's acquaintance and was, so to speak, his contemporary, came into my ken the other day by means of a bundle of letters belonging to a descendant of his employer; and the perusal of his correspondence makes him a living character—conscientious, precise, devoted to his business, and content with the active little world of Edinburgh. I think of him as a small, stout man, his brow furrowed with minor worries, his eyes turned rather apprehensively on the doings of the politicians and the generals and their possible effect on prices and taxes; in whom political upheavals and the threat of foreign war or domestic rebellion usually produce the bewildered comment, 'What all this will turne to God only knowes.'

His name was James Nasmyth, writer in Edinburgh. From about 1720 to 1750 he acted as 'doer' for Alexander Murray of Broughton, a Galloway laird living at Cally, near Gatehouse-of-Fleet. This Murray was no relation of that other Murray of Broughton who came of a Peeblesshire family and earned an unenviable immortality as 'Mr Evidence Murray' by his behaviour after the 'Forty-five. Alexander Murray represented an old family in the Stewartry of Kirkcudbright. His father had married the heiress of the Lennoxes of Cally, and apparently left Alexander very comfortably off, with an estate to which he added by considerable purchases of land. His marriage to Lady Euphemia Stewart, daughter of the fifth Earl of Galloway, seems to have increased his fortune and his responsibilities. He also owned property in Ireland, granted to his great-grandfather by James VI. Accordingly a great deal of business provided material for a frequent correspondence between the laird of Broughton and his doer.

But estate management and enlargement are not the only topics of these letters. The distance of Galloway from Edinburgh, and the notorious badness of country roads before the days of Telford and outwith the operations of Wade, made the Murrays' visits to Edinburgh very rare events, and the commissions entrusted to Nasmyth made him much more than a mere law-agent. He carried out every kind of charge for his employer, from engaging servants to getting watches mended. A new top for Broughton's cane, a writing-desk for his son, a case of oranges, a pair of Communion cups, glassware, cloaks, wigs, and walnuts are among the articles which Mr Nasmyth is directed to procure and despatch to Galloway. It is a striking commentary on the difficulties of transport in George II's time that 'a wryteing desk and drawers for Mr Murray, 200 weight common barley, 100 weight pearl barley, and a stone weight millet seed' were sent by ship from Leith, presumably all the hazardous way of the Pentland Firth and the Minch. Lighter goods were sent by carrier, sometimes to their hurt, like the 'chest of oranges' entrusted to John Walls, the Dumfries carrier, in February, 1734. 'I charged him', wrote Mr Nasmyth indignantly, 'to forward the fruit with the utmost dispatch least they should spoyle by lying. But there is no trusting these fellows.'

Another of this hard-worked man's responsibilities was to keep his employer supplied with reading matter. 'Wee have a new paper published here', he writes in the same month as the unlucky affair of the oranges; 'I send you one for a specimen. If you lyke it you may be furnished with them weekly.' Again:

'You have by the bearer a book upon improvements said to be wryt by Provost Lindsay [the Lord Provost of Edinburgh], and a pamplet which takes it to peices reckoned to be wryt by Lord Grange and another newly publish't at London. They are all new and may give some amusement when you have a leisure hour.'

Sometimes the books and pamphlets he sends throw an interesting light on the composition of a country gentleman's library. 'Please also receive the *Edinburgh Almanack* for the present yeare, the Advocat's *Letter to a Bishop*—this was a weighty pamphlet on the fashionable Hutchinsonian theology from the pen of Duncan Forbes of Culloden—'and another little book just published and in great vogue for countrey use, together with the Political Works of Fletcher of Saltoun bought for you some tyme agoe.' The appearance of the second volume of Bishop Burnet's *History of his Own Time* (ten years after the first) is also noted: 'I shall send your copy with some very curious pamphlets lately come downe by the first opportunity that offers.'

The management of Broughton's affairs brought Mr Nasmyth into contact with some eminent lawyers. Charles Erskine of Barjarg, later Lord Tinwald, who rose to be Lord Justice Clerk, was often consulted; and so was Alexander Lockhart, afterwards Lord Covington, that energetic and brilliant advocate who threw himself into the affairs of his clients with such enthusiasm that, as a contemporary notes, 'he seemed to think he could not do enough for them'. It is strange to find how cheaply the services of such a man could be obtained in those days.

'Mr Lockhart came to toun Saturday evening' (reports Nasmyth in May, 1741). 'I waited on him yesterday, laid your whole papers before him which I perused with him one by one allong with a memoriall and queries which I had before taken from them, and thereafter left all with him till this evening when I got them back with his signed opinione of the whole . . . together with a scroll of the disposition . . . which is also perused and signed by him and me as you order.'

Such rapidity in business might be expected of a man who egularly sat down to his desk soon after four o'clock in the morning, but it is startling to find Nasmyth diffidently adding, 'I gave him three guineas, observeing he was att a great deal of pains, which I am hopefull you will approve of.'

But that was an age when an eminent professor's salary might be no more than £70 a year, and a minister's stipend much less. At the other end of the scale we find Nasmyth, in 1734, describing a prospective footman as 'extravagant in his wages' because 'he will have no less than £5 [a year] besides twenty shillings of the house drink money'. Although the candidate was 'a sightly neate fellow and as I am told sober', with 'ane exceeding good character', Nasmyth finally engaged for the Murrays another applicant—'young but seems abundantly smart and I am told is very sober'—at only '£3 per annum of wages and twenty shillings of the house drink money and his charges to the countrey'.

When business matters were despatched, Nasmyth filled up his letters with public news. There are echoes in his letters of Frederick the Great's Silesian campaigns, of Admiral Vernon's disastrous West Indian expedition in 1740–1, when Tobias Smollet served as surgeon's mate on board the *Cumberland*, of the threatened French invasion in 1744, and of Walpole's fall and the beginning of Pelham control in Parliament. Political gossip is frequent, whether from 'above', as Nasmyth generally calls the distant arena of Parliamentary battles, or from Scottish constituencies, where the families of Dundas and Hope and Erskine were beginning their rise to political eminence. He has a keen eye, too, for the probable effects of Government's doings on his employer's affairs: 'the Commons have voted 20,000 seamen for the service of the year, and if the land forces bear a proportion wee may expect a swingeing Land Tax.'

Here and there in these letters stirs the dust of long-forgotten controversies. Lord Grange, that talented, hypocritical bundle of twisted ambitions, refusing to be kept out of Parliament by Walpole's statute excluding Scottish judges from it—aimed deliberately at him—resigns his judge's gown to return to the bar and enter the Commons as M.P. for Stirling burghs. 'Mr Erskine of Grange', reports Nasmyth, 'now shynes att the bar as he always did on the bench when he had a mind to it and is exceeding throng in bussiness.' Another letter, of 10 March 1734, refers to the suspension of the Rev. Ebenezer Erskine from his charge at Stirling, as a result of his uncompromising attitude against the system of patronage in the kirk. On the day appointed for the intimation of the sentence, 'the mob got up as it's said to the number of 4,000 and neither the magistrats nor the military thought fit to medle with them, so the thing is undone. What all thir things may turne to' (comments Mr Nasmyth as usual) 'God Almighty knowes.'

Their ultimate result, for one thing, was the formation of the Secession Church, first known as the Associate Presbytery.

General news in Nasmyth's letters, apart from political events, includes what might be called an intermittent gossip-column concerning society in the capital. He chronicles marriages and deaths, and notes in particular the movements of Lord Stair, perhaps the most eminent man in Scotland in the 1730's with the exception of the Duke of Argyll, and plainly the object of his admiration. Some of his news reminds us that Scottish society, in spite of the Union, still centred in Edinburgh.

The spring of 1734 was full of activity. 'Thursday evening' (writes Nasmyth on 23 March) 'the Duke and Dutchess of Queensberry aryved att their lodgeing in Cannongate. The Duke of Buccleugh is to be att Dalkeith this night. A great many others of the nobility are expected here so that in appearance wee shall have a gay summer.'

The Duke of Atholl is appointed Lord High Commissioner to the General Assembly, 'who are lyke to have warm work'. The Duke of Marlborough comes north, 'for whose receptione Pinkie House it's said is fitting up'; and Robert Dundas of Arniston, destined fourteen years later to succeed Duncan Forbes as Lord President of the Court of Session, is entertained by the freeholders of Midlothian at the end of April in the cramped old Assembly Room in the West Bow, 'where after dinner they gave him their solemne thanks for the good service he had done the natione in generall, this countie in particular, and beg'd of him to stand for their member now with assureances of adhæring to him as one man.'

Mr Nasmyth did not, save on professional errands, move among the *élite* of Edinburgh legal society, and he lived before the great days of Edinburgh clubs, when lords and *literati*, advocates and agriculturalists, mingled in the convivial gatherings of the Cape, the Select Society, or the Poker Club. His only recorded acquaintance of interest to us to-day was William Adam the architect, the father of the famous Adelphi brothers. In 1742, when Adam was at the height of his powers and reputation, and had already built the Edinburgh Royal Infirmary, Alexander Murray toyed with the notion of employing Adam to design him a new house, and Nasmyth was instructed to approach him. 'He tell's me', reported the doer, 'that the least he ever had when called att such a distance to make out a plan of a house is twenty guineas and that free of charges out and in.' Incredible as it appears, Broughton seems to have thought this modest charge excessive. In a later letter Nasmyth assured him that Adam was 'far from being a money catcher', adding with unconscious irony that 'on the contrair he is very often bitt by bargains he makes'. Matters hung fire, however, and at the end of September, though Nasmyth 'conversed him att great length over a glass of wyne', Adam could not be persuaded 'to goe att this season of the yeare on the terms you are pleased to mentione'. As the new house of Cally

was not built till Alexander Murray had been thirteen years in
his grave and Adam fifteen in his, it remains uncertain whether
its handsome design was Adam's or not.

More interesting, perhaps, than the long-vanished glitter of
Edinburgh society of 200 years ago are the glimpses of what
Mr Nasmyth saw and heard discussed as he went about his
business or dallied at the old Mercat Cross of Edinburgh,
where the merchants and the lawyers met at noon to discuss
the affairs of the city and the state beneath the crowned tower
of St Giles, scattering the music of its chimes above the narrow, malodorous streets and the smoke of their crowded
chimney-pots. The sudden death of Lord Daer is one topic of
conversation, 'of a dead palsie as they call it,' after he had
danced himself into a fever at an Edinburgh ball: 'the old
Earle is inconsoleable, he being his only sone.' A severe epi-
demic of something like influenza strikes the city in January,
1742, 'occasioned, I reckon, by the extraordinary variableness
of the weather, and so many of our Lords [of Session] are confined that this day they were obleidged to rise as soon as set for
want of a quorum, a thing I never remember to have knowen
before'.

The death of a great landowner has its repercussions. 'Duke
Hamilton is either dead or dying att Bath . . . which must be a
loss to the countrey as he spent his estate in it.' The price of
meal is up or down, and the probable effect on trade of a
reported cruise of the French fleet is gravely discussed.

The excitement of the Porteous riot and its sequel would
have given Mr Nasmyth much to write about, but unfortunately his letters of 1736–7, like those of 1745–6, are missing.
The most thrilling event he actually describes is the fire of
May, 1741, which did 'incredible damneage' and destroyed the
family papers of the Craufurds of Crosbie. On this, like other
happenings, Mr Nasmyth looks with a strictly professional eye.

Through all his correspondence, Mr Nasmyth appears a diligent and devoted servant of Broughton's interests, and writes
painstakingly voluminous accounts of all his proceedings. One
story which continues by instalments for several months con-

cerns a search in the Laigh Parliament House (now part of the National Library of Scotland) for an old charter of the lands of Broughton, 'where the lands are disigned a barrounie'. The quest goes on from December, 1733, to April, 1734, and is at length abandoned after it has ranged 'from the [year] 1300 to 1600 without finding any thing that can be of use. I am sorry for the expence,' adds the good man, 'as it happens to be throwen away'; and he reminds his employer of 'the records having been caryed to London during the usurpatione', when 'above thrity tun of them were cast away att sea when comeing home after the Restoratione'. An extract from the records costs, he reports, 'no less than 120 merks tho' it's but a sheet of paper.' No wonder that he remarks later of the Parliament House, 'I have ane aversion att going there because of their exorbitant fees'.

The fire of 1741 and the shocking loss of Mr Ronald Crawfurd, W.S., determine Mr Nasmyth to prepare against any similar accident. 'I have caused make a strong box of wainscot with iron bars,' he writes in February, 1742, 'in which I keep all your papers, which I hope you'l approve of.' In August he assures his employer: 'Whatever comes of me, all will be found together and in good order.'

His letters show that he was completely trusted by the Murrays, and their style is sometimes a curious blend of subservient formality and easy intimacy. Every one begins with the words 'Honoured Sir', and ends with the usual ceremony of the period; yet what comes between is sometimes almost chatty, and he more than once refers to his wife, evidently in allusion to some joke between himself and his employer, as 'the waefull woman'.

He outlived Alexander Murray by nearly four years, dying on 8 February 1754 at the age of sixty-four. Their connection had lasted for at least thirty years, and only once does it seem to have been ruffled. This was in November of the year 1743, when Nasmyth took it into his head that his employer had spoken slightingly of him to an acquaintance and cast doubts on his professional honesty.

'This' (he wrote bitterly) 'is not the ordinary way people of your rank take with their doers. If you meane by it you are wearie of my service let me know and you shall have no paine for you are never to lose a shilling by me.'

Yet even this indignant missive begins and closes as usual with 'Honoured Sir' and 'Your most obedient humble servant'. A mollifying reply brings his apology.

'If any thing unguarded hath escap't me I beg, Broughton, you'l lay it where it certainly is—to my weakness and the surprize this incident gave me which would have affected a man of more fortitude than I. . . . Your very good letter of the 11th makes me quite happy as it frees me from the anxiety I have been under least by my owne rashness I should have given ane interuptione to a correspondence which I have always considered as one of the greatest blessings of my life.'

8

'WORTHY NAIRNE':
LORD DUNSINNAN

About six miles north-east of Perth rises the high and conspicuous hill of Dunsinnan. A prehistoric fortress on its oval top, surrounded by a rampart of large stones bedded in clay, was in the eighteenth century supposed to be the remains of the strong castle built by Macbeth on the advice of the weird sisters. A few miles to the west of it was the moor they were believed to have frequented, where the country people pointed out 'the witches' stone'. Close to it stood an 'elegant mansion-house', the seat of Sir William Nairne, second baronet of Dunsinnan.

Sir William, who was the head of a family settled in Perthshire since the days of Robert III, had been twice married, in each case to a widow. By his first wife he had a son named Thomas, born in 1708, and two daughters; the only child of his second venture—Emilia Graham, daughter of David Graham of Fintry and widow of a Hunter of Burnside[1]—was a son whom he named after himself. Sir William died at Scone on 26 June 1754 at an advanced age, leaving Dunsinnan to his elder son Thomas, now a married man with a family. His other son, William, was studying for the law in Edinburgh, where, on 11 March 1755, he was admitted a member of the Faculty of Advocates.

He seems to have been a quiet but pleasant enough young man, welcome in Edinburgh society, given to mild academic jests, and regarding life with a realistic and unimaginative eye.

[1] National Library of Scotland MS, 37:2:4.

His friends appear to have belonged mostly to the legal profession which he now entered. Many young men of good family passed advocate simply for the value of a legal training in politics or in estate management or merely for a broadening of their education.[1] Thus admission to the Faculty carried with it admission to a wide and not only professional circle.

Among Nairne's friends were the energetic and humorous George Dempster of Dunnichen, a young Angus laird who had been admitted to the Faculty a week before himself, and his close companion Adam Fergusson, who entered it the following December. The correspondence of these three sheds a little light on Nairne's character and tastes at the age of about 25.

Dempster had started with Fergusson in the spring of 1756 to perform the grand tour; but family affairs called him home after six months. He returned to Edinburgh to dazzle his friends with his new French clothes, bearing their chaff good-humouredly and retaliating at the expense of their more sober dress. On 5 December 1756 he wrote to Fergusson in Brussels:

'I must own a little surprise to return to a country without

[1] Thirty years before, Professor Alexander Bayne had addressed his first year students in the class of Municipal Law at Edinburgh University with the argument: 'But besides, gentlemen, you will consider what an ornament it is to know the law of your country. Is there any thing more frequently the subject of conversation, or which bears a greater part in it, than the cases that daily occur in law? . . . And, on these occasions, is it not a mark of distinction for a gentleman to be able to acquit himself tolerably? . . . Let us but consider, then, the knowledge of our law, as the proper embellishment of a gentleman, without regard to the useful part; and does it not even in that abstracted light deserve your application? But when we consider it as an useful ornament, pray, gentlemen, what more agreeable personage can one form to himself, than that of a country gentleman, living decently and frugally on his fortune, and composing all the differences within the sphere of his activity, giving the law to a whole neighbourhood, and they gratefully submitting to it?'—*A Discourse on the Rise and Progress of the Law in Scotland*, appended to Bayne's edition of Sir Thomas Hope's *Minor Practicks*, 1726, pp. 186–7.

nobility, and where the law predominates and triumphs over
the sword, and a set of people who are but ranked in the second
class every where else, the first and most considerable here; to
find a man pass for a gentleman without a laced coat or diamond ring, and to hear from Nairne that he had been visiting
Lady Boyde in a valet de chamber's frock and an unpowdered
brown greezy head. . . . Nairne watches my motions with all
the vigilance of a Mentor to take care that none of 'em betray
affectation, conceit, or a contempt of the homely objects that
surround me.'[1]

Nairne saw much of Dempster during the next year or two.
Often, with another friend, Robert Arbuthnot,[2] they sat up
half the night, discussing the world's affairs and putting them
straight with the usual confidence of youth. Home rule for
Scotland was a topical subject in those days as in ours; but in
1757 the model admired by Scottish Nationalists was not Ireland nor Denmark—but Switzerland. Dempster wrote:

'In discourses of this kind the sun often surprises us. Often
have we disolved the unequal union of our country to England,
converted it into a republic, marshal'd Scotia's warlike sons,
cultivated her barren fields, fortified her avenues and strong
places, and reestablished her long lost independence.'[3]

Neither Dempster's reminiscences nor Fergusson's letters
roused in Nairne at this time any wish to travel himself. Scotland was evidently good enough for him. Writing to Fergusson
on 30 May 1757 he says:

'I hope you will find in Italy all the satisfaction and entertainment which you expected to have there. . . . I can't say I
envy your enjoyments, but I wish I was with you to share
them, tho' I so far take part in your concerns, that what makes
you happy gives me pleasure, even at so great a distance. I'm
afraid you will repent leaving so fair a country as by all

[1] *Letters of George Dempster to Sir Adam Fergusson*, pp. 15–16.
[2] An Edinburgh merchant (d. 1803) who was in later life Secre-
tary to the Board of Trustees for Fisheries, Manufactures, and
Improvements in Scotland.
[3] *Letters*, p. 32.

accounts Italy is, to return to the rugged hills and frozen climate of your native Caledonia. Let me assure you that our snows are not constant, nor our atmosphere continually filled with showery clouds. At this moment our sun shines as bright as where you are and gently warms us while it broils you. We had what is called a hard winter, that is a very frosty one, which I think the wholsomest and best, and a very favourable seed-time gives us now the hopes of a plentiful harvest.'

He sent his absent friend some literary news from Scotland. John Home's new tragedy 'Douglas', produced with tremendous *éclat* at Edinburgh five months before, had at last achieved the stage of Covent Garden. 'The reverend author', wrote Nairne, 'is to demit his charge and from such encouragement will I dare say continue to write. I'm hopeful he will do credit to his country, as he really has a very fine genius.' David Hume had published the second volume of his *History of Great Britain* and had pleased the critics this time, 'for he has not laid himself open to the censure which the first justly incurred, from the indecent contempt of religion which he there showed'. He had also published some 'dissertations . . . elegant, ingenious and philosophical. In all his works,' added Nairne regretfully, 'he shows himself so acute and master of such talents that it is really deplorable so great abilities should be so ill employed and that a mind so capable to discover truth should have so fatal a byass to error.'

How much more commendable were the poetic labours of Mr William Wilkie, the eccentric and rustical minister of Ratho! He had just published his epic poem, the 'Epigoniad', in which the most searching eye could not discern the smallest danger of originality. Nairne had read it with 'keenness and curiosity' and thought well of it.

'I really think it a fine thing, it's extremely like Homer. . . . The plan is not perhaps unexceptionable, but his poetic fire is equal to Homer's (who in that has hitherto remained unrivalled), his similies are no less frequent, and in my opinion not inferiour.'

Nairne's friendship with Dempster continued to the end of

his life; but with Fergusson, though their tastes and opinions had much in common, he seems to have lost touch.

In November, 1762, he and Dempster made the acquaintance of young James Boswell, at Paxton's inn in the Grassmarket. Boswell's journal records his first impressions of them both. Dempster he found 'a most agreeable well-bred man, sensible and clever, gentle and amiable, quite a gentleman'. Nairne he set down as 'an honest upright fellow; somewhat stiff in his manner, but not without parts in a moderate degree'.[1]

Nairne and Boswell met again in the Netherlands the following year, when Boswell was in his turn performing the grand tour. Boswell found his acquaintance 'just the old man, quiet, sensible, worthy'; and 'Worthy Nairne' is again the description that Boswell applies to him in 1767. His journal records many friendly meetings in their own and other people's houses during the 'sixties and 'seventies.

Nairne devoted himself to the law with more assiduity than any of these three friends of his, being appointed Commissary Clerk of Edinburgh in 1758, conjointly with his uncle Alexander Nairne, and later becoming Sheriff of Perthshire. Sir Adam Fergusson (as he had become on his father's death in 1759) practised at the Bar for some years with success; but Dempster gave up the law to go into Parliament in 1760, and Sir Adam followed him to Westminster in 1774, while Boswell, having hovered for some time between the Bar and the Army, made, after 1763, the pursuit and cultivation of Samuel Johnson the chief end of his life. In 1773 he persuaded that formidable critic of the Scots to test his opinions of them by firsthand observation, and Nairne was one of the earliest of his Edinburgh acquaintances to be introduced to Johnson on the latter's arrival in Edinburgh. This was on the second evening of Johnson's first stay in the capital, when Nairne was invited to supper at Boswell's house in James's Court on the north side of the Lawnmarket. When the two travellers set out for the north Nairne accompanied them as far as St Andrews.

[1] *The Private Papers of James Boswell*, vol. i, pp. 125-6, 130.

Johnson liked Nairne, with his quiet manners and his fondness for the classics, and their conversation was amicable. When they were about to embark to cross the Firth of Forth, Boswell pointed out to Johnson that 'the port here was the mouth of the river or water of Leith', and Nairne added with a smile, 'Not *Lethe*'.

'Why, sir,' said Johnson, 'when a Scotchman sets out from this port for England, he forgets his native country.'

'I hope, sir,' retorted Nairne, 'you will forget England here.'

'Then 'twill be still more Lethe,' replied Johnson vigorously, and went on to deprecate the unnecessary size of the pier— 'you have no occasion for so large a one: your trade does not require it.'

They landed on Inchkeith, where Johnson let his fancy play, as he did more than once on the islands he visited, with the notion of building a house there. Then, resuming their passage, they proceeded to Kinghorn, where they dined, and took a post-chaise for St Andrews. They travelled by Kirkcaldy and Cupar, Johnson and Boswell in the chaise, and Nairne and Boswell's servant Joseph riding beside it. They had 'a dreary drive, in a dusky night' to St Andrews, but Johnson 'revived agreeably' at Glass's inn. Nairne introduced his companions to Dr Watson, a professor at the University, with whom they lodged; they found their host 'a well-informed man of very amiable manners'.

Nairne accompanied his two friends during a part of their exploration of the little city, where they were entertained, as Johnson put it, 'with all the elegance of lettered hospitality'. Yet a certain gloom oppressed them at the spectacle of 'an university declining'—it had at this time fewer than a hundred students—'a college alienated, and a church profaned and hastening to the ground'; and Johnson assailed the memory of Knox with whole-hearted abuse. Nairne himself shared the Englishman's feeling of depression. As they paced the cloisters, Johnson's booming voice echoing portentously from the old walls while he 'talked loudly of a proper retirement from the world', Nairne remarked that he himself 'had an inclination to retire'. Johnson gave a qualified approval to this wish, holding that a man might withdraw himself from the world without blame when he had 'done his duty to society', and backing his opinion with a line of Hesiod.

Nairne was in Edinburgh (for the time of the Session was approaching) when Johnson and Boswell returned there from Auchinleck after the conclusion of their Highland tour. He accompanied them on a visit to the Castle, which Johnson admitted to be 'a great place', and a few days later entertained them to supper at his own house, near the Parliament Close. He undoubtedly left a pleasant impression on the mind of Johnson, who recorded their travelling together on the first page of his *Journey to the Western Islands*, with a courteous reference to Nairne as a 'gentleman who could stay with us only long enough to shew us how much we lost at separation'. When the book was published, Nairne was among the first of Johnson's Edinburgh acquaintances whose good opinion of it Boswell was anxious to ascertain. 'Went home with young Donaldson,' says his journal on 12 February 1775, 'and got the *Monthly* and *Critical Reviews* on Mr Johnson's 'Journey', which were a feast. . . . Found Mr Nairne when I came home, and read the reviews on Mr Johnson to him.'

On 12 April of the following year Boswell invited Nairne to dine with him at the Crown and Anchor tavern in London, to meet Johnson, Sir Joshua Reynolds, Bennet Langton and an old friend, Sir William Forbes of Pitsligo. As might have been expected with such a company, it was an evening of lively conversation, and Johnson talked memorably of drinking, of his *Rambler*, of reading in general, of Fielding's *Amelia*, Cumberland's *Odes*, and the *Reviews*; but if Nairne attempted to compete in conversation with the wit and wisdom around him, he said nothing that struck Boswell as worth recording, even as a foil to Johnson.

He does not appear, indeed, to have shone much in conversation, though Boswell found enough amusement in one or two of his remarks to note them in his commonplace-book. He was not unsociable. He would hardly have been a friend of Boswell's if he had been, nor would he have been—as he was—a member of that lively body of Edinburgh wits and *literati*, the Poker Club. Yet he was a quiet man, and his temperament was a solitary one—a quality perhaps due in some measure to the background of his childhood and early youth, with no male relations but a half-brother old enough to have been his father, and a father who might have been his grandfather.

The wish to retire from the world of which Nairne spoke to Johnson in 1773 was probably no affectation; for he had had many private troubles to bear. Sir Thomas, his half-brother, had died in 1760, and the owner of Dunsinnan was now his son, Sir William Nairne, the fourth baronet, whose brother Charles had also died, in India, where he was in the East India Company's service, in 1771. Nairne's mother had died in 1767, at Bridgeton. He himself, although the heir-presumptive to the family estate, never married. Yet loneliness was easier to bear than the fearful scandal caused in 1765 by the trial of his niece Katharine for the murder of her husband.

Katharine Nairne, a spirited and reckless young woman, with 'a high nose, black eyebrows, and a pale complexion',[1] had been married in January, 1765, at the age of nineteen, to a middle-aged laird of a sickly constitution, Thomas Ogilvie of Eastmiln, who lived with his mother in a small and unattractive house in Angus. It was perhaps not very surprising that Katharine heartily disliked the match. But to poison her husband with arsenic four months after marrying him was a somewhat excessive expression of her distaste for him; and to her contemporaries it was still more shocking that she should have done so with the help of her husband's brother Patrick, a lieutenant in the 89th regiment, with whom she was alleged to have fallen passionately in love within a week of the wedding. They were both arrested, tried, convicted and condemned to death. Katharine was defended by the warm-hearted, eloquent and emotional Alexander Lockhart (afterwards raised to the Bench as Lord Covington), the diligent advocate who had

[1] So described in the Edinburgh magistrates' proclamation for her apprehension.

been 'att a great deal of pains' for Alexander Murray of
Broughton twenty-five years before, and who was by now
Dean of the Faculty of Advocates. He made tremendous efforts
on her behalf. The trial lasted for forty-eight hours, and one of
the judges, Lord Auchinleck, was taken dangerously ill with a
strangury through remaining on the Bench for nine hours
without a break during the examination of a key witness.
Lockhart 'displayed such powers of·eloquence and ingenuity
as astonished everybody', and appeared unaffected by the
strain, though his opponent, the Lord Advocate, was completely worn out. 'To save the life of his unhappy client, he
gave up, with great art, her character, but contended that
there was no legal proof of her *guilt*, though enough to damn
her fame.'[1] His skill, his persistence and his oratory were alike
unavailing, and Katharine was condemned to suffer with her
paramour.

Patrick Ogilvie's situation—for he, too, was young—aroused
more public sympathy than Katharine's, and strong efforts
were made to save his life. He was reprieved more than once,
and devoted the anxious time of waiting to playing on his
violin. But at length, on 13 November 1765, he was duly
hanged, after some rather horrible bungling, in the Grassmarket. Katharine pleaded her pregnancy, and her execution
was delayed.

The case had stimulated enormous public interest. Katharine, like Madeleine Smith nearly a hundred years later, did not
lack defenders, and the arguments for and against her guilt
were freely discussed in Edinburgh society. The grief and
shame of her uncle did not prevent his resolving at all costs to
save his niece from the gallows. A lawyer himself, he could not
be ignorant of the impropriety of his interfering with the
course of justice. None the less, there is every reason to believe
that Katharine's escape from the Tolbooth was made with his
connivance and probably by his invention. She slipped out of
the prison one evening disguised as the midwife, Mrs Shiells,

[1] *Scotland and Scotsmen in the Eighteenth Century*, vol. i, p. 134,
note.

SIR WILLIAM NAIRNE, LORD DUNSINNAN
From the portrait in the Parliament House, Edinburgh,
by Sir Henry Raeburn

who had been attending her, and who for several days had passed the gaoler with her head muffled up on the plea of toothache.

On the evening of 15 March 1766, Katharine muffled her own head in the same manner, walked boldly out of the prison, and made her way to the foot of the Horse Wynd, where a carriage was waiting. In it was James Bremner, her uncle's clerk. A male disguise was provided for her, and under Mr Bremner's escort Katharine was hurried south to Dover, whence she escaped to France. Her uncle had given Mr Bremner the grim instruction that if pursued along the coast road they were to drive into the sea that Katharine might drown herself rather than be taken alive. But all went according to plan, though Mr Bremner had some most uncomfortable moments during the journey owing to the frivolous behaviour of his charge, who was so excited at her escape from the Tolbooth that, as he complained afterwards, 'she was continually putting her head out of the window and laughing immoderately.'[1] Judging from her behaviour in Scotland, the legend that she subsequently married a Dutch gentleman, had a large family, and lived happily ever afterwards, seems on the whole more credible than the report that she spent many years in a French convent, and died in England some years after the French Revolution.[2]

No scandal attached itself to William Nairne, and he continued to follow the law with very fair success. 'If he did not acquire the fame of a great orator or a profound lawyer, he was at least respectable in both capacities.'[3] He amassed a moderate fortune, and was at length able to buy the family estate from his nephew Sir William Nairne, who, lacking the interest, the capacity, or perhaps merely the money to modernise

[1] *Kay's Edinburgh Portraits*, 1877, vol. ii, p. 219.

[2] Mr William Roughead's imaginative reconstruction, in the R.L.S. manner, of Katharine Nairne's escape ('Lord Dunsinnan's Spectacles' in *The Rebel Earl, and Other Studies*, 1926), loses a good deal of conviction by his portraying her uncle as an old judge instead of the advocate of about 35 he actually was.

[3] *Kay's Edinburgh Portraits*, vol. ii, p. 217.

and improve it as had become necessary, was probably not unwilling to pass it on to an uncle with a keen interest in agriculture. The price Nairne paid was £16,000, and when he entered into possession of Dunsinnan he had practically no ready money left. He set himself to live as economically as possible until he should find his funds sufficiently increased to carry out the agricultural reforms on which he had set his heart.

On 27 February 1786 he was raised to the Bench, and took his seat in the Court of Session on 9 March. The Duchess of Gordon complimented him on his promotion with a pun which it must have taken all her celebrated vivacity and charm to pass off as wit. Meeting him soon after his appointment, she asked him by what name he was now to be known. 'Dunsinnan,' replied the judge. 'I am astonished at that, my Lord,' replied the Duchess, 'for I never knew that you had *begun* sinning.'[1]

A pun of Nairne's own, preserved by Henry Mackenzie, the author of *The Man of Feeling*, is more subtle. An acquaintance of Nairne's ran over a pig in his carriage and killed it. 'I am surprised,' remarked Nairne, 'that so good and pious a man should have committed *suicide*.'[2]

Some years after his elevation to the Bench Lord Dunsinnan sat to Henry Raeburn for a portrait which afterwards passed into the possession of the Faculty of Advocates. It hangs to-day in the Parliament House in Edinburgh, in a conspicuous position next to the door by which you enter that historic hall from Parliament Close. Although the paint is cracked and yellowed and much in need of cleaning and restoration, the picture has a charm which draws the eye. Lord Dunsinnan leans back in his chair with an air of satisfaction. He looks contented and at ease. From under fine black eyebrows his gaze twinkles at the strolling advocates, the hurrying messengers, and the visitors casually loitering round the portraits and

[1] Kay's *Edinburgh Portraits*.
[2] *The Anecdotes and Egotisms of Henry Mackenzie*, ed. H. W. Thompson, 1927, p. 111.

statues that line the walls, with an expression half kindly and half cynical. He looks like a man who has reached the top of his tree but found nothing there to excite him: a man who has seen much of life but never found cause in it for either complacence or despair, a man whose emotions have never run to extremes. His face is quietly humorous, genially deprecating. The one thing you cannot call it is dull.

Very different is the face etched by John Kay. Raeburn portrayed the judge in a pose of relaxation, still in his robes, but at the end of his day's work on the Bench. Kay drew him still on the Bench, the geniality hidden under a blank mask, the white-gloved hands decorously folded, heavy-lidded eyes turned slightly upward with an expression almost sanctimonious. It is a striking contrast.

In 1790 Lord Dunsinnan's nephew died at the early age of 45. He had been married, since 1769, to Alexandrina Scot, fifth daughter of Robert Scot of Dunninald, who survived him till 1820; but they had had no children. The judge succeeded him as fifth baronet of Dunsinnan. His finances were still feeling the strain of purchasing the estate, and by his promotion his professional income had become limited to a fixed salary. He continued to live with the strictest economy. At Dunsinnan, where he spent the legal vacations, he kept only a small household, and invited no guests. Not unnaturally he was accused of parsimony. Perhaps there was some foundation for the charge. A story was told of a visit paid to him by George Dempster, now retired from Parliament but as busy and sociable as ever. The visit was intended for only a few hours, but late in the afternoon a violent storm broke, and Dempster dropped a hint to his host that he might have to remain all night. Dunsinnan became extremely agitated. The fact was that he had only one bed in the house—his own—apart from the servants'. He did his best to deflect Dempster, as politely as possible, from his purpose of remaining; he hoped against hope that the storm would abate enough for his guest to reach Perth at least; and at length even went out himself to the stable to order Dempster's carriage to the door. But here he found himself defeated by Dempster's coachman, who flatly refused to harness his horses in such weather to face the notoriously bad roads of the district,[1] and declared that he would rather lie on straw in the stable till morning if he could get no better lodging. Lord Dunsinnan returned in despair to his guest and explained the difficulties of the situation.

'George,' he said, 'if you stay, you will go to bed at ten and rise at three; and then I shall get the bed after you.'[2]

In spite of these domestic privations, Lord Dunsinnan was able to proceed with the improvement of the estate. In his zeal for agricultural reform he resembled many of his brethren of the Bench, such as Monboddo and Gardenstone, Kilkerran and Kames before them, and Kilkerran's son Hermand in later years. The real revolution of Scottish agriculture had reached its zenith earlier in the century; but at Dunsinnan methods were still old-fashioned, and the laird laboured earnestly to bring them up-to-date. The run-rig system still prevailed at his accession, with all its inconvenience and waste, and the 'outfield' of the farms, which the tenants held gratis and so had no inducement to cultivate, produced no crop but heather and rough grass. Dunsinnan set to work to make radical reforms. He divided his land into regular farms, allotting a certain proportion of outfield to each, and induced the farmers to enclose the barren land and cultivate it. He encouraged them to grow turnips, potatoes and flax, besides the traditional oats and barley, and to follow a proper rotation of crops. By 1798 he had managed to build a number of good modern farm-houses. The increase of the population in the parish of Collace (where Lord Dunsinnan was the sole landed proprietor) was ascribed in the *Statistical Account of Scotland*[3] to 'the encouragement given by the proprietor to farmers and tradesmen of every denomination'.

Dunsinnan had passed his seventieth birthday soon after the beginning of the century, and on 8 August 1808 he resigned

[1] See Robert Southey: *Journal of a Tour in Scotland in* 1819, ed. C. H. Herford, 1929, p. 26.

[2] *Kay's Edinburgh Portraits*, pp. 217–8.   [3] Vol. xx, p. 237.

his appointment as a Lord of Justiciary which he had held since December, 1792. Robert Dundas (Lord Melville's son) wrote in acknowledging his letter of resignation:

'Directions have accordingly been given for preparing forthwith a warrant for the appointment of Lord Hermand as your successor, and I have also taken measures for expediting the warrant for the pension authorised by the late Act of Parliament.'[1]

Dunsinnan still found it necessary to husband his money carefully in order to carry on the development of his estate. He saw no reason to waste any of it by falling in with the suggestion of Sir John Sinclair of Ulbster, that indefatigable framer of 'projects', that he should erect a monument on the top of Dunsinnan hill in commemoration of Macbeth's castle. His evasion, dated 6 September 1808, was polite but firm:

'Although I am not sure if the fine green top upon the black hill, which affords evident marks of manual labour and habitation, would receive much embellishment from anything that could be built upon it, yet I should willingly give my consent to any gentleman, who thought it would be ornamental to the country, to make such an erection as you should approve of, because I am sure it would be in the best taste; but, as to myself, the truth is, that I have been laying out so much of my money in the valley, that I really could not at present afford anything to the hill.'[2]

In 1809 Lord Dunsinnan resigned from the Court of Session altogether; his letter of resignation was written on 31 January.[3] The last few months of his life were spent in the rural quiet of Dunsinnan. George Dempster, who now generally lived at Broughty Ferry or St Andrews, 'playing golf, whist, and the fool,' as he said,[4] tried to induce his old friend to visit him. In March, 1811, he persuaded himself that Lord Dunsinnan would come to Broughty Ferry during the approaching summer, and

[1] National Library of Scotland MS 59 (Melville Papers), f. 109.
[2] *The Correspondence of Sir John Sinclair*, 1831, vol. i, pp. 458–9.
[3] National Library of Scotland MS 59, f. 163.
[4] *Letters of George Dempster to Sir Adam Fergusson*, p. 338.

wrote some jubilant doggerel to celebrate the success of his
endeavours:

> *Posterity will all agree*
> *That, when compared with you and me,*
>> *Old Orpheus is but noughty:*
> *He brought a girl*
> *To the door of hell—*
> *We've drawn a hermit from his cell*
>> *At Dunsinnan, to Broughty.*[1]

But his satisfaction was premature. A fortnight later, on 23
March 1811, Lord Dunsinnan died. He bequeathed his estate
to his great-grand-nephew James Mellis, descended through
the female line from Sir Thomas Nairne; the baronetcy became
extinct.

Lord Dunsinnan left behind him a happy and prosperous
community of thriving farmers and busy craftsmen. The prosperity he had brought to the estate had doubled and even
quadrupled the rents of the farms, but the people of Dunsinnan
had reaped its principal benefits. The land was well cultivated,
the new plantations were flourishing, the people were well
housed, and every old or infirm person on the estate had a
cottage and garden rent free. One of Dunsinnan's last projects
had been the building of a new parish church, 'a handsome
Gothic structure,' but it was not finished till the year after his
death.[2] He himself was buried within the walls of the old
church. He had followed Dr Johnson's advice, and done his
duty to society before retiring from the world.

[1] *Letters of George Dempster to Sir Adam Fergusson*, p. 333.
[2] *New Statistical Account of Scotland* (Collace), vol. x, p. 212.

9

THE FARMER JUDGE:
LORD HERMAND

I

The name of George Fergusson, Lord Hermand, is chiefly
known to the modern reader from the writings of Lord Cockburn and the anecdotes recorded by Maidment and Paterson
which accompany the drawing of Hermand in *Kay's Edinburgh
Portraits*. It is quite natural that such memorials should have
fastened on him the reputation of an eccentric, for the subjects
of Kay's art were generally selected for their oddity, and Cockburn, although one of the most amiable of men and most
charming of writers, was inclined to exaggerate the peculiari-
ties of the men he described, particularly when their politics
were opposed to his own.

I shall have occasion to quote from Lord Cockburn a great
deal. He knew Hermand in his old age intimately, was con-
nected with him by marriage, and had a deep affection for him.
His descriptions are vivid and his testimony valuable. But it is
important to remember that just as Raeburn in his later portraits displays his sitters in dramatic poses and under an almost
melodramatic light, so Cockburn's strong sense of comedy and
equally strong prejudices sometimes distort the images of the
great legal figures he describes in a way which does him more
credit as a literary artist than as an historian. Mr William
Roughead has shown that Cockburn's portrait of Braxfield is
far from just and greatly exaggerates the alleged coarseness
and callousness of his character.[1] A part of my task in this

[1] See 'The Real Braxfield' in *Glengarry's Way*, 1936.

essay is to prove that Hermand should not be solely remembered for those qualities which are pre-eminent in Cockburn's sketches of him in the *Memorials of His Time*, *Journal*, and *Circuit Journeys*: 'intensity of temperament', 'diverting public explosions', and above all 'a sincere respect for drinking, indeed a high moral approbation, and a serious compassion for the poor wretches who could not indulge in it; with due contempt for those who could, but did not'.[1]

Two outstanding qualities of Hermand's character, which Lord Cockburn passed over, were his intense family loyalty and his abiding interest in the political concerns of his native county of Ayrshire. To appreciate these, a fuller knowledge of his earlier life is necessary than Cockburn probably possessed. A background of home, heredity and family life must be sketched for a proper understanding of the figure on which Cockburn fixes our attention.

George Fergusson was born on 25 August 1743 and baptised the same day.[2] His birthplace was his father's house of Kilkerran, in the wooded valley of the Water of Girvan in Carrick; and it was there and in Edinburgh that he grew up, as one of a closely united and affectionate family circle.

Lady Jean Fergusson, a pious and kindly woman and a devoted mother, was adored by her children. Long after her death, in the General Assembly of 1805, Lord Hermand made, during a hotly contested debate, a typically passionate speech which showed how lively to him was the memory of his mother, even after forty years.

' "Sir! I sucked in the being and attributes of God with my mother's milk!" His constant and affectionate reverence for his mother exceeded the devotion of any Indian for his idol; and under this feeling he amazed the House by maintaining (which was his real opinion) that there was no apology for infidelity, or even for religious doubt, because no good or sensible man had anything to do except to be of the religion of his mother; which, be it what it might, was always the best. "A

[1] Henry Cockburn: *Memorials of His Time*, 1856, pp. 132–4.
[2] Dailly Parish Register.

sceptic, Sir, I hate! With my whole heart I detest him! But, Moderator, I love a Turk!" '[1]

George was the youngest but one of Lady Jean's fourteen children, and one of the eight who survived the dangers of an eighteenth-century childhood. The brothers and sisters among whom he grew up were the following: John, the eldest, who died of consumption, to the great grief of his parents, before George's seventh birthday; Adam, who ultimately succeeded his father, and who seems to have been George's special intimate, though ten years older—perhaps because they both adopted the law as a career; Charles, who became a wine-merchant in London and was the father of Sir James Fergusson, later fourth baronet of Kilkerran; James, who died a planter in the West Indies in 1778; and three sisters, Jean, Margaret and Helen, the last of whom became, in 1770, the second wife of Sir David Dalrymple, Lord Hailes.

When in Edinburgh, the family occupied a dwelling in Forrester's Wynd, known as Kilkerran's Court. It seems to have been slightly cleaner and more comfortable than most of its neighbours in that insanitary district, since Lord Kilkerran once advertised it to let at the unusually high rent of £20 a year, recommending it as 'free of bugs and smoke'.[2] Lord Kilkerran also had what Lady Jean called 'a little neat house' at Sunberry, near Edinburgh, known as 'the Windmiln'. It was there that he died in 1759.

The first few years of George's childhood were passed at Kilkerran. The alarms of the Jacobite rising made it seem a safer place than the capital, and even after that had been quelled Lady Jean and her children seem to have spent more time there than in Forrester's Wynd, where quarters must have been considerably cramped for so large a family. In the improvement made to the family estate is some explanation of the passion for farming which seized on George Fergusson when, late in life, he too became a landed proprietor. Not only

---

[1] Cockburn, *Memorials*, p. 208.
[2] Chambers's *Traditions of Edinburgh*, vol. ii, p. 235; also quoted in Graham's *Social Life in Scotland in the Eighteenth Century*.

must he have seen and heard discussed, during the first fifteen years of his life, the improvements on which his father spent so much time and attention, but during his middle life he cannot have failed to notice, on every visit to Kilkerran, the progress which his brother was making in carrying on their father's work.

It is proper to add that another of Lord Hermand's recreations, hard drinking, was also hereditary. Lord Kilkerran, though he was considered by the standards of the time an abstemious man,[1] must in the middle course of his life have been as confirmed a devotee of claret as George became; for his son Adam testified, more than forty years after his death,

'If any person of his time of life had been asked who the man in Scotland most afflicted with the gout was, the universal answer would have been Lord Kilkerran. In fact, though I was five and twenty years old when he died, I do not remember ever to have seen him able to walk farther than his own garden.'

In the winter the family probably went to Ayr, 'where almost all the families came from their country-houses to spend the winter in routs and assemblies,' and where such neighbours as John Hamilton of Bargany and Sir John Whitefoord of Blairquhan had town houses for that season.[2] When they went to Edinburgh they probably travelled by Strathaven and Hamilton, and the journey took at least two days, generally more. They were at 'the Windmiln' during John's last illness in the summer of 1750, and in the early autumn of 1751, before Lord Kilkerran started on the autumn circuit, they were taking the water at Duns, perhaps on account of Lord Kilkerran's gout.

[1] Ramsay of Ochtertyre records a saying about the Lords of Justiciary at this time—'that there were two of them, Justice-Clerk Erskine and Minto, who *ate*; two of them, Strichen and Drummore, who *drank*; and two that neither ate nor drank, Elchies and Kilkerran.'—*Scotland and Scotsmen in the Eighteenth Century*, vol. i, p. 93, note. But v. *supra*, p. 55, Lord Auchinleck's anecdote on Lord Kilkerran's drinking habits.

[2] John MacDonald: *Memoirs of an Eighteenth-Century Footman*, ed. by John Beresford, 1927, p. 27.

Lady Jean's account-book provides details of the family's life in Edinburgh during the years following 1753, when George's elder sisters were old enough to take part in the amusements of the capital. Peggy, the second daughter, died in October of that year of consumption, but Jean and Nelly, Adam, who came of age in May 1754, and Charles, then 14, found Edinburgh full of entertainment, with balls and assemblies, plays at the Canongate Theatre, Allan Ramsay's circulating library, Mr Piscatori's concerts, and domestic music of their own making as well—Adam had a fiddle and the girls played the spinet and the virginals.

Adam meanwhile was studying for the Bar, and the younger boys were receiving tuition from private teachers. Mr Dallas came to teach them to sing, and Mr McCulloch, for a fee of thirty shillings a quarter, taught them 'to write and count'. Dr Stevenson, the family physician, attended them when they were ill, and Dr Young was paid ten shillings 'for blouding George and Jamy at different times'. 'Losenges and squill mixture', particularly the latter, were the usual remedies for minor ailments. But things were more serious in the winter of 1754–5 when 'Jamy had the small pox and George and Jamy the measles', and ass's milk had to be got for them at a cost of £2, 8s. 6d., with a fee of a further 2s. 'to the servant who milked the ass'—probably brought for the purpose to the door of the house in Forrester's Wynd.

Other items in the accounts for 1754 are 'shoes for Charles, George and Jamy', 'a yard linnen for nightcaps to George', and 'a book to George'. On 30 December appears an entry of four shillings for the 'children's hansel'—the New Year present which George and his brothers probably spent, like young Henry Cockburn a generation later, in the Krames, 'a low narrow arcade of booths, crammed in between the north side of St Giles' Cathedral' and the Luckenbooths, which 'contained everything fascinating to childhood, but chiefly toys'.[1]

In 1755 Mr Corser succeeded Mr McCulloch as 'writeing master for George and Jamy', and Mr Murdoch was paid a

[1] Cockburn, *Memorials*, pp. 108–9.

guinea a month for 'teaching childern french in the house'. 'Maps bought by Mr Thomson for the use of the childern learning geography' cost 7s. 6d., and on 17 April Mr Moffat, glass-grinder, charged thirteen shillings 'for makeing up the glass of the little parlour which George broke'.

The entry of 2s. 'to George to buy a Horace for the school' on 24 June 1755 indicates that he was proceeding to a fresh stage in his education. He was probably accompanied to school by his brother Jamy, for they both got a quantity of new clothes during this summer, their mother's purchases including 'twelve yards and three quarters of linen for six shirts to George and Jamy at two shillings and three pence per yard', 'rufles to George and Jamy', and 'black cravats to George and Jamy'.

The school to which George was sent was regarded as one of the best in Edinburgh, and from about 1740 to 1760 was kept by Mr James Mundell, a teacher of such distinction that after his death 'out of respect to him, a club was formed, consisting of those who had been his scholars. . . . The members were in the habit of dining together at stated periods in honour of his memory. At these social meetings the parties lived their boyish days over again; and each was addressed in the familiar manner, and by the juvenile *soubriquet* which he bore when one of the "schule laddies". Any deviation from these rules was punished by a fine.'[1]

This is perhaps the first recorded specimen of an association of 'Old Boys' or 'F.P.'s', and seems to have had some of the characteristics of its successors.

Among George's contemporaries at Mundell's school were Claud Boswell, a nephew of Lord Auchinleck, who was in later years to be his colleague on the bench as Lord Balmuto, and David Erskine, second son and heir (since the death of his elder brother, Lord Cardross, in 1747) of his father, the tenth Earl of Buchan. As eleventh Earl of Buchan he was to blossom into one of the ripest eccentrics of the Edinburgh of Sir Walter Scott's time, and to be the founder of the Society of Anti-

[1] *Kay's Edinburgh Portraits*, 1877, vol. i, p. 298.

quaries of Scotland. Others who attended the school were the future Lord Polkemmet; Andrew Hunter, later minister of the Tron Kirk and Professor of Divinity in the University of Edinburgh; and a second cousin of George's—though possibly unacknowledged as such—Caleb Whitefoord,[1] afterwards celebrated in London as a journalist, satirist and poet. (Caleb was a natural son of Lord Kilkerran's cousin, the gallant Colonel Charles Whitefoord who was taken prisoner at Prestonpans after fighting Cope's artillery single-handed when all the gunners had run away.) A school with such a list of pupils gave an excellent introduction into the Edinburgh world in which George was to spend so much of his professional career.

In the winter of 1756–7, when his brother Adam, who had passed advocate a year before, was making the Grand Tour, George entered the University of Edinburgh, in the Logic and Metaphysics class of Professor John Stevenson. He continued this study for three years, adding to it Humanity, under Professor George Stuart, in March 1757, and Greek, under Professor Robert Hunter, in March 1758.[2]

Adam returned home in the summer of 1758 after two years on the Continent, and seven months later, on 20 January 1759, Lord Kilkerran died at the age of 70. The house at 'the Windmiln' was sold to Lord Glencairn,[3] and Lady Jean apparently retired to Kilkerran. Sir Adam contemplated entering Parliament, and accepted an invitation from the Town Council of Ayr to stand for Ayr burghs at the next General Election; but Lord Loudoun and Lord Bute, who had other plans in view for this seat, persuaded him to withdraw.[4] He turned to the Bar and soon made his mark there. It may have been his example or advice, as much as the recollection of Lord Kilkerran's

[1] *The Whitefoord Papers*, ed. by W. A. S. Hewins, 1898, p. 267.

[2] Edinburgh University Records, *ex inform.* Dr L. W. Sharp.

[3] Sir Adam Fergusson to Alexander Cuningham, 25 April 1760: Laing MSS, Edinburgh University Library.

[4] See *English Historical Review*, January 1937: *The General Election of 1761 at Ayr*, by W. L. Burn. There is much material concerning this transaction among the unpublished Bute and Loudoun MSS.

distinguished career, which moved George to begin studying for the Bar in 1763.

Before this time, however, he had at least one other interest, of which I have found no trace in his later career. In the room at Kilkerran next to the old dining-room there hangs on the panelled walls a set of little landscape drawings with the signature 'Geo. Fergusson delin., 1760'. They are conventional in style, and appear to be copies or imitations of French and Dutch engravings, but they are done with a skill which shows a real application and devotion to the art.

However, in 1763 George returned to the University and entered the class of Civil Law under Professor Robert Dick, going on to Municipal Law the following year under Professor John Erskine. On 17 December 1765 he was admitted a member of the Faculty of Advocates.

II

I have found no record of George Fergusson's life during his early years at the Bar. His mother died in 1766. Of his brothers, Sir Adam was in steady practice as an advocate, and his name is prominent in the proceedings of the Douglas Cause, when he drew up the Hamilton memorial, and in the Sutherland succession case, in which his client—Elizabeth, Countess of Sutherland—was his second cousin, Sir Adam and Sir David Dalrymple (his future brother-in-law) being two of her five guardians. Charles, after a few years in Madeira, had established himself in business in London as a wine-merchant, and had married in 1764; his elder son, James, afterwards Sir Adam's successor, was born the following year. The youngest brother, Jamy, found no career until, some years later, he became a planter in Tobago, where he died in December, 1777, after two years of hard work, having sunk in unsuccessful plantations of coffee and indigo a good deal of Sir Adam's money.

In 1774 Sir Adam Fergusson entered Parliament as member for the shire of Ayr, and it is at this election that George Fergusson's name first appears on the roll of electors for that constituency. As he owned no property in Ayrshire he was not, of course, properly entitled to a vote, but by a common legal subterfuge, which was becoming something of a scandal during the last half of the eighteenth century, he acquired what was called a 'nominal and fictitious' vote by receiving sasine from his brother of a small property of the requisite rental. The roll of Ayrshire freeholders rose from 97 names at the Michaelmas Head Court of 1759 (when Sir Adam's name first appeared therein) to no less than 235 at the by-election of 1781, and from 1774 the name of 'George Fergusson of Polquhirter' figures among the qualified voters and generally among those who actually recorded their votes.

In the early 1770's George's home in Edinburgh seems to have been in Milln's Square, but in 1774 he was living in Hyndford's Close—a convenient distance from the Parliament House. Sir Adam's Edinburgh house was in the more salubrious quarter of St Andrew Square, a recently built and very fashionable district, where his neighbours included his cousin Sir John Whitefoord (the son of the Sir John Whitefoord previously mentioned), a pompous, dapper little man who had been a major in the Army and fought at Minden; Andrew Crosbie, a famous character among Edinburgh advocates who is supposed to have been the original of Counsellor Pleydell in *Guy Mannering*; and William Pulteney, M.P. for Cromarty, a Johnstone of Westerhall who changed his name on marrying the wealthy heiress of the Earl of Bath. Hamilton of Bargany and David Hume lived just round the corner.[1]

George was a member of the Poker Club, of which a full account may be found in the *Autobiography* of Dr Alexander Carlyle, and also belonged to the *Ante Manum* Club, of which his friend Charles Hay, later promoted to the bench as Lord Newton and immortalised in paint by the brush of Raeburn, was the principal pillar. Its chief end was just drinking—it owed its name to the rule that the bill should be paid *beforehand*—and according to Cockburn, who passed a few uncomfortable evenings with the last survivors of it, it 'contained,

[1] Williamson's *Edinburgh Directory*, 1773–4.

and helped to kill, most of the eminent topers of Edinburgh'.
The meetings took place every Friday for six or seven months
in the year, and when George Fergusson was in his Bacchan-
alian prime 'he used very often to go direct from the club to
the Court on the Saturday mornings'.[1]

No one ever hinted that drinking, however late or heavily,
impaired in the slightest degree George Fergusson's professional abilities. Dean Ramsay calls him 'a capital lawyer' in the
same paragraph as that in which he speaks of his many 'convivial meetings' with Charles Hay;[2] and Lord Cockburn insists
that 'no carouse ever injured his health, for he was never ill, or
impaired his taste for home and quiet, or muddled his head:
he slept the sounder for it, and rose the earlier and the cooler'.[3]

A fondness for good wine, a love of good company, and a
keen interest in Ayrshire politics were three points George had
in common with another Ayrshireman whose head for liquor
was not so strong as his own: James Boswell. Their families
had been long acquainted, but the Fergussons got on better
with Lord Auchinleck than with his volatile son. George Fergusson is mentioned several times in Boswell's journals as
dining at Lord Auchinleck's—for the first time on 7 July 1769,
when Boswell records of himself 'I was dull enough, but contented to be so'.[4] At Auchinleck, on 15 October 1776, Boswell
notes, 'Mr George Fergusson came to breakfast. His keeness
[sic] pleased me. Lord Hailes and he went to Ballochmile'[5]—
the residence of Sir John Whitefoord. A year later, on 21
October 1777, George Fergusson dined and spent the night at
Auchinleck with some other company, and Boswell records
dismally, 'Whist. No conversation.'[6] There is, however, a
rather fuller reference to George on 2 February 1779 when
Boswell heard in Edinburgh a false rumour of his father's

[1] Cockburn's *Memorials*, pp. 224–5.
[2] *Reminiscences of Scottish Life and Character*, 1924 edition, p.
181.
[3] *Memorials*, p. 135.
[4] *Private Papers of James Boswell*, ed. by F. A. Pottle, vol. viii,
p. 42.
[5] *Op cit.*, vol. xii, p. 60.   [6] *Op cit.*, vol. xiii, pp. 70, 71.

death. 'When I came to the Court,' he writes, 'I saw Mr George Fergusson and several people arround him looking surprised and concerned. I asked him what it meant. I shall not forget the affectionate appearance which he had when he said to me, "I am told your Father's dead." '[1]

But Boswell and Sir Adam Fergusson were never on very good terms; and as Sir Adam retained the Ayrshire seat in Parliament, the winning of which was Boswell's dearest ambition, intermittently for nearly twenty years, Boswell's attitude towards him became increasingly hostile. It was not therefore to be expected that George Fergusson, whose loyalty to his brother was one of his outstanding characteristics, would be very intimate with James Boswell.

In 1775 was published the collection which Lord Kilkerran had made of the decisions of the Court of Session from 1738 to 1752—the year in which the Faculty of Advocates appointed a committee to make an official compilation of the decisions of the Court. Lord Kilkerran's book, of which Lord Kames's biographer remarked that it 'exhibits the clearest comprehension of jurisprudence, and will for ever serve as a model for the most useful form of law reports,'[2] has for long maintained Lord Kilkerran's credit as a legal authority, and the editing and publishing of it, although the preface says that the Decisions are 'published nearly as he left them', must have been a not inconsiderable task. The title-page announces that the book is published 'by his son', and it is generally accepted that the editor was Sir Adam Fergusson. I hazard the guess that it was in reality his brother George. Sir Adam, having just fought an election and gone into Parliament, can have had little time on his hands for the work, and George's own collection of *Consistorial Decisions* (first published by the Stair Society in 1940) shows that such an editorial task would have been to his taste. If evidence may be drawn from the preface or 'Advertisement', it can be maintained that its style bears far more resemblance to the abrupt and pithy manner of George's surviving corre-

[1] *Ibid.*, p. 198.
[2] A. F. Tytler: *Life of Lord Kames*, vol. i, p. 36.

spondence than to the polished and rather long-winded periods of his brother's.

It was in November of this same year (1755) that George received his first legal promotion, when he was appointed one of the Commissaries of Edinburgh in place of James Smollet of Bonhill, Sheriff-Depute of Dunbartonshire, who had died on 12 November.[1] Boswell had apparently been in hopes of getting this post himself. He was supping at Sir George Preston's on 25 November, and 'George Webster was there. He told that George Fergusson was appointed one of the Commissaries of Edinburgh. This was a small dissapointment to me.'[2] George took his seat as a Commissary on 6 December,[3] and it may have been about this time that the idea occurred to him of compiling a digest of the decisions of the Consistorial Court of Edinburgh.

In 1777 he played a part in a ridiculous dispute which had attracted some attention in the society of Glasgow. In 1775 a quarrel had arisen between two gentlemen, Captain David Peter of Crossbasket and Mr James Tennant of Annfield, regarding the possession of a small-sword which was the property of a Glasgow merchant named Harry Horseburgh. Captain Peter had borrowed the sword from Horseburgh to keep up his appearance during a visit to Portugal, but omitted to return it. It appears that he was rather in the habit of forgetting to return things which had been lent to him. At last Horseburgh and his friend Tennant took an opportunity of visiting Peter's house and removing the sword; it was Tennant who actually took it, but he carried it away in Horseburgh's company.

Captain Peter was furious and accused Tennant of theft or 'spuilzie'. Ignoring the fact that the sword was not his, he raised a process in the Sheriff Court of Lanark against Tennant. His case was that he had had the sword for ten years, and that as Mr Horseburgh had never asked for it back presumably he did not mind Captain Peter's retaining it; if Mr

[1] *Scots Magazine* (1775), vol. xxxvii, p. 637.
[2] *Private Papers of James Boswell*, vol. xi, p. 18.
[3] *Scots Magazine, loc. cit.*, p. 640.

Horseburgh wanted his property again he should have asked for it in a regular way, and Tennant had no right to take it out of Peter's house. The Captain prayed therefore that Tennant 'should be ordained to deliver to the petitioner the sword above mentioned, with the sheath thereof, or to make payment of the value of the same, with damages and expenses, etc'.

The Sheriff, not unnaturally, found that the sword was Mr Horseburgh's property and dismissed the process. So much might be expected, as also his decision that no expenses were due on either side. What was less orthodox, though very human, was his pronouncement that the parties in the dispute were 'censurable for the illiberal strain of the debate', and his fining them five shillings each 'for behoof of the poor'.

Peter paid his fine, but was not disposed to let the matter rest there. He pursued the case, and in February 1777 it came before Lord Braxfield, with Henry Erskine as counsel for the petitioner. Braxfield had little sympathy with Peter's complaint, and on 20 February he pronounced a brief interlocutor:

'Having considered the debate, suspends the letters *simpliciter*, and decerns: Finds the charger liable in expenses and allows an account to be given in.'

The implacable Captain pursued the matter further, and gave in a petition to the Lords of the Inner House. The counsel who had been retained for Mr Tennant was George Fergusson, and a part of his speech on his client's behalf has fortunately been preserved. It shows that he was fully alive to the humours of the case, and to the opportunity for an ironical demolition of Captain Peter's fantastic claim:

'My Lords, it is not supposed that your Lordships will incline to appoint the respondent, Mr Tennant, to give up the sword to Captain Peter, in order that it may in the next place be delivered to the real owner. Even supposing that the sword was in Mr Tennant's possession, it would be rather easier to make him give it to the owner himself; but when it is admitted that Mr Horseburgh has it *already*, Mr Tennant frankly owns that it passes his comprehension to conceive what it is that the petitioner, Captain Peter, would have your Lordships' order on the respondent to do. Surely he will hardly desire that you should appoint it to be delivered up, in order that he may keep it to himself, for he admits that it does not belong to him, neither will he desire your Lordships to appoint it to be delivered up, in order that it may be restored to Mr Horseburgh, for this very satisfactory reason, *because Mr Horseburgh has it already!*'

If George did not quote a good maxim of Scots law—'He quha makis lauchful retribution of the gudis may not be callit for spuilzie,' the Lords may well have had it in mind. They affirmed Lord Braxfield's interlocutor, with expenses. Captain Peter was left with his grievance, and Mr Horseburgh with his sword.[1]

In 1780 George Fergusson's interest in Ayrshire politics shows itself in some of his earliest surviving letters. A General Election was approaching, in which Sir Adam Fergusson would have to defend his seat in Parliament against a representative of the family of Eglinton whose power he had challenged when he won it six years before. His opponent this time was to be Major Hugh Montgomerie of Skelmorlie (afterwards twelfth Earl of Eglinton), and it was clear that the fight would be a close one. 'Nominal and fictitious' votes had been manufactured on both sides in large numbers: there had been 124 names on the roll of freeholders at the Michaelmas Head Court held just after the election of 1774, but by the time the electors came to the poll on 16 October 1780 they numbered 206.

A letter which George Fergusson wrote to John Davidson, W.S., on 24 April 1780 (now in the Laing MSS in Edinburgh University Library) is the earliest though very far from the only evidence of the keen interest which George took in his brother's political contests and of the way in which he acted as a kind of electioneering agent for him in Edinburgh. In August he went to Kilkerran to give his assistance on the spot, and on the last day of that month accompanied Sir Adam to Kilmar-

[1] *Glasgow Past and Present*, 1884, vol. iii, pp. 296–304.

nock, where they met James Boswell, between whom and Sir Adam a coolness had now developed. Boswell wrote in his journal:

'Met Sir Adam Fergusson on the street; shook hands with him and was polite but reserved. . . . His brother George was there too.'[1]

It is rather implied that the reserve extended to George also, although the previous year Boswell and he had been friendly enough.[2]

In September George attended the Circuit Court at Ayr. The Circuit judges were Lord Kames and Lord Braxfield, and it was then that George heard Lord Kames sentence to death an old acquaintance and former opponent at chess, named Matthew Hay, with a brutal joke upon the jury's verdict of Guilty—'That's checkmate to you, Matthew!'[3] At the end of the month he was still at Kilkerran and deep in his brother's election business. Sir Adam had assured Henry Dundas at the beginning of the month that 'everything is secure in Ayrshire', but writing to 'Fish' Craufurd of Auchinames on the 10th he considered his success 'not now certain. It is only highly probable.' At the election on 16 October 55 electors, including his brother George, voted for Sir Adam, and 60 for Major Montgomerie. The efforts of both candidates to disqualify each other's votes had evidently been extremely successful; but there were so many accusations and counter-accusations of illegal voting that the whole matter was gone into first by the Court of Session and later by a committee of the House of Commons, which finally declared Sir Adam elected.

Meanwhile Boswell, who had had to return to Edinburgh, was waiting eagerly for news of Major Montgomerie's success, and recording with a kind of shocked satisfaction a remark

[1] *Private Papers of James Boswell*, vol. xiv, pp. 106–7.

[2] Charles Rogers: *Boswelliana*, 1874, p. 286.

[3] The remark has been ascribed to Braxfield, but Cockburn 'had this fact from Lord Hermand, who was one of the counsel at the trial, and never forgot a piece of judicial cruelty which excited his horror and anger' (*Memorials*, p. 117).

about George Fergusson made by the learned but cantankerous John Maclaurin (afterwards Lord Dreghorn):

'No news as yet of the Ayrshire election. . . . As McLaurin and I walked home, he said he wished Major Montgomery success, for he liked him, and he hated George Fergusson and "would crack him like a louse". He maintained that a man who was not vindictive had no warmth of freindship. He "would not ride the water on him". For his part he never forgave. "Curse your enemies," said he with keeness.'[1]

These savage utterances, apparently inspired by George Fergusson, may surely be taken as evidence of the conspicuous activity he must have shown during the General Election in Ayrshire.

He came over to Ayr again to record his vote on 8 August 1781, at the by-election necessitated by Sir Adam's appointment as a Commissioner of Trade and Plantations, when the latter retained the seat. Three years later George accompanied his brother—apparently as a witness—when he rode from Kilkerran to King's Well, between Kilmarnock and Glasgow, to conduct a prolonged argument with Sir John Whitefoord, who had taken offence at not being consulted about the plan Sir Adam had formed with Henry Dundas to turn over the Ayrshire seat to Montgomerie, receiving Edinburgh city in exchange. The brothers were quite unable to pacify Sir John. 'At going away,' wrote Sir Adam afterwards, 'I held out my hand to him; but he withdrew his, so we parted.'

Sir Adam having become M.P. for the city of Edinburgh on 31 August 1784, he and George must have seen more of each other than usual during the next few years. It is unlikely that Sir Adam ever attended a meeting of the 'Crochallan Fencibles', that cheerful gathering whose meetings Burns so much enjoyed during his stay in Edinburgh; but George's friend Charles Hay, being one of its most prominent members, may have introduced his fellow-advocate to it. There is no record, alas! of George's having encountered Burns there or elsewhere. Both he and Sir Adam, however, added their names to the sub-

_____
[1] *Private Papers of James Boswell*, vol. xiv, p. 137.

scription list for the first Edinburgh edition of Burns's poems which appeared in April 1787.

III

Sir Adam remained a bachelor all his life, and George himself did not marry till after his fiftieth birthday. The wife he chose was a first cousin once removed, some eighteen years younger than himself. Her name was Graham (or Graeme) MacDowall, and she came of one of the oldest families in Scotland, the MacDowalls of Garthland, while on her mother's side (Elizabeth, daughter of James Graham of Airth) she was descended from the great Marquis of Montrose. Her father was William MacDowall, second of Castlesemple, in Renfrewshire, and fifteenth of Garthland. He had acquired Garthland, the original home of the MacDowalls in Galloway, from his first cousin of the same name, the fourteenth laird of Garthland, who had died childless in 1775 and was the elder son of Alexander MacDowall, thirteenth of Garthland, the husband of Lord Kilkerran's sister Jean. The present owner of Garthland and Castlesemple was Graham's brother, another William MacDowall, M.P. for the Glasgow burghs, who had, so to speak, kept the Ayrshire seat warm for Sir Adam in 1789–90.

George's marriage took place on 23 December 1793.[1] Although Mrs Fergusson's name occurs fairly often in the family correspondence she is a somewhat shadowy figure, no letters of her own having survived. Lord Fullerton, her nephew by marriage, described her as 'the ideal perfection of a judge's wife',[2] and her obituary notice in the *Edinburgh Evening Courant* speaks in flowery terms of her virtues:

'In a wide circle of honourable connections and acquaintances, she secured universal esteem by her benign disposition and engaging manners. . . . To the afflicted poor of an extensive parish and neighbourhood she was an unwearied benefactor, and it is the testimony of no partial relative, that her kindly sympathies, liberal charities, and Christian counsels, will long

[1] *Scots Magazine* (1793), vol. lv, p. 619.
[2] Lord Strathclyde: *Lord Fullerton*, 1921, p. 38.

be remembered in many an upland and village home, as her enlightened conversations and courteous attentions will be by numbers in that superior situation in society in which she was placed.'

Three years before his marriage George had been living at No. 31 Princes Street,[1] but before long he and his wife planned to make their home in the country. Whether it was now or later that what he called his 'passion for farming' seized upon him, the locality in which they decided to live was certainly not chosen either for attractive scenery or a sociable neighbourhood. It was a property called Herdmansheills in the parish of West Calder: a flat, dreary-looking countryside about twelve miles south-west of Edinburgh. George bought it from Robert Balfour of Balcurvie, and took sasine of his new estate —'Herdmansheills, Heugh-head, and that part of Sclateheugh called Dykefoot'—on 16 July 1796.[2] There was no house on the property. The house of Hermand, which still stands materially unaltered, a square, unpretentious, comfortable-looking building, with large rooms opening on to a central well round which the stair rises, appears to have been built in the course of 1797.[3] George and his wife were certainly living in their new home, which already bore the name of Hermand, by March 1799. A walled garden was laid out beyond the burn which flowed at the back of the house.

It is uncertain when the family zeal for improving land broke out in George Fergusson, but it was certainly the cause, soon after the purchase of his estate, of an important change in his life. He had for some years been talked of as a candidate for the Bench. The Duke of Portland, writing to Robert Dundas, the Lord Advocate, in 1796, mentioned that the latter's father, Henry Dundas, who was an old friend of both George and Sir Adam, had 'suggested the propriety of offering the double gown to Mr George Fergusson, and after him, but with a sort

[1] Williamson's *Edinburgh Directory*.

[2] H.M. Register House, Edinburgh Sasines, 412: 35.

[3] Rev. J. M. Wilson, *Imperial Gazetteer of Scotland*, n.d., vol. i, p. 224.

of qualification which seemed to place him, though next, *longo intervallo*,[1] he mentioned Mr Honeyman.'[2]

The Advocate had sounded George on the subject, but he did not seem anxious for the proffered honour. It is to this approach that George refers in writing to Sir Adam from Edinburgh on 18 March 1799.

'Two years ago, I declined accepting the place of the last Justiciary judge that died, Lord Abercromby,[3] on account of several cases which I wished to plead, some of them in the House of Lords. But Mrs Fergusson, who was then against my accepting it, has begun to change her mind, and I do not know but I am somewhat in the same situation myself, as I feel rather sore, at being obliged to leave my farming operations to write law papers, which I have been under the necessity of doing just now, after having been at Hermand for a week. I would be glad however to have your advice upon the subject, and to know how you think I ought to proceed in either view.'

A factor which had probably weighed with George in favour of becoming a judge, and against the disadvantage of a reduction of income, was the long vacation which offered to a judge 'six months of freedom' in the year, with 'the utter cessation of business, the long truce, the mind's recovery of itself, the relapse into natural voluntary habits' which Lord Cockburn, whose passion was gardening, found so infinitely refreshing.[4]

Sir Adam's reply to this letter has not survived, but it evidently suggested that George should drop a hint in the proper quarter that his views had altered. But this George felt reluctant to do, as he explained in another letter, also from Edinburgh, about 30 March, when he frankly acknowledged that his enthusiasm for farming was the chief reason for his change of mind.

---

[1] *'Proximus huic, longo sed proximus intervallo.'*—Virgil, *Æneid*, v. 320.

[2] Historical MSS Commission, Laing MSS, vol. ii, p. 585. Honeyman became Lord Armadale.

[3] He had died in November 1795.

[4] *Journal of Henry Cockburn*, 1874, vol. i, pp. 110, 112.

'I know not if it be wise, but what has the chief effect in leading me to feel somewhat differently from what I did a little more than two years ago, when Lord Methven got the Justiciary gown, vacant by the death of Lord Abercromby, is the passion I have contracted for farming, which is a good deal interrupted by *vacation* papers, generally the most important and tedious, upon which I have been obliged to employ the last ten days, with the necessity of returning to them some little time hence. But I learned from you long ago, and have always felt, that it was not decent to sollicit being employed in judging on the lives and fortunes of others. I know indeed, my situation is so far different from what sometimes occurs, as the Advocate made me the offer, very handsomely, when Lord Abercromby died, and it may be thought that I have only to withdraw a bar, which I myself then created. But even this does not quite remove my scruple, and unless somebody else brought on the subject, I feel I myself could not do it. Your advice however will always have the greatest weight with me, and certainly has confirmed what I have of late been beginning to think.

'There does not seem to be any great hurry in the business, for as I really do not see an individual whom it could be very desireable to bring into the Court of Session, so you know that it is only a judge of that Court that can be made a Commissioner of Justiciary, and therefore no individual can be brought from the *bar* sooner than the Court meets upon the 12th of May, though no doubt one of the present Lords of Session might at any time be brought into the Court of Justiciary. If that however was vacant, why is it not already done?

'If you had an opportunity of seeing Mr Dundas, you could easily say, that you had advised me to agree to a change of situation, and you found me disposed to do so. The question is, if the same thing could be written, without the appearance of what I really could not bear in such a case, that of making interest, or employing sollicitation, for what ought to be conferred, and never sollicited.'

Sir Adam had retired from Parliament in 1796, but his politi-

cal influence in Scotland was still considerable, so that any
request of his to Dundas was certain to be heard with attention, apart from the claims of long friendship and the known
worth of his character. It was natural, therefore, to suggest
that he should act as an intermediary. The matter was further
discussed between the brothers in Edinburgh during the spring,
and Sir Adam wrote to Dundas from Ayr on 27 May, recalling
the circumstances in which George had been offered promotion
in 1796.

'I can now gather that the reasons which influenced his
declining the proposal at that time have ceased to operate; and
I have reason to think that if the same opening occurred again,
he would accept. I told him I thought he should write to you,
or to the Lord Advocate, to let this be understood. But I find
he has an objection to doing so, which he says he learned from
me; I having it seems some time or other mentioned my
opinion, that it was a delicate thing to solicit so responsible an
office as that of a judge. Be that as it will, and whatever my
conduct would be with respect to myself, I think I need have
no scruple in letting you know the present state of his mind. I
do not do so however by way of soliciting for him even at
second hand; but merely to let you know that if he should be
thought worthy of the situation, it would not probably now be
declined.'

The hint would probably have been sufficient by itself, for
George Fergusson, being a true-blue Tory at a time when,
according to Lord Cockburn, Whig lawyers had 'every official
gate shut against them',[1] was undoubtedly 'thought worthy'.
Politics apart, his ability and integrity were well known. But
in the meantime he had so far overcome his scruples as to
make assurance double sure by himself speaking to the Lord
Advocate. His letter to his brother of 30 May explaining this
betrays a very human mingling of the delicate and the business-like.

'DEAR BROTHER,—Though I take it for granted that you
would write to Mr Dundas, as you proposed, from Ayr, yet as it

[1] *Memorials*, p. 92.

was the Advocate, who two years ago offered me, in the handsomest manner, the Session and Justiciary gowns, then vacant, I thought it right to mention to him, that I no longer had the objection to accepting them, which I then stated—that I did this, not in the way of sollicitation, which I considered as improper in the case of such offices, but merely in order to show that my objection was withdrawn.

'He said that on every vacancy since, I had been mentioned by the Chancellor and Mr Dundas, but that he had reminded them of my refusal; and asked if I would take the *single* gown for the present. I answered that I could not acquiesce in so great a diminution of my present income, and that I could not accept of the one without the other. This he is to communicate to Mr Dundas, though he could not say any thing positive himself.

'The poor Justice Clerk died yesterday,[1] and Eskgrove succeeds him. This with Lord Swinton[2] makes *two* Justiciary gowns vacant, as well as two in the *Session*, for you will have heard that Lord Monboddo is likewise dead. He is to be succeeded by Claud Boswell,[3] so that if they choose it, there is room enough for me.'

Sir Adam received this letter on 2 June 1799, and in reply sent his brother a copy of the letter he had written to Dundas. There was no need for them to do anything further, but George's ambition to secure the Justiciary gown as well as the Session one was not realised: he did not attain it for nine years. However, he was appointed a Lord of Session in the room of Lord Braxfield on 4 July, and took his seat on the bench on 11 July by the title of Lord Hermand. John Anstruther was appointed one of the Commissaries of Edinburgh in his place.[4]

[1] The date of Lord Braxfield's death is given in more than one reference book as 30 May instead of 29 May. His obituary notice in the *Scots Magazine* (May 1799) gives the correct date.

[2] Lord Swinton had been dead since 5 January.

[3] As Lord Balmuto.

[4] J. P. Wood's *Records of Judges and Advocates* (National Library of Scotland MS 37.2.4, f. 144); *Scots Magazine* (1799), vol. lxi, p. 492.

THE FARMER JUDGE: LORD HERMAND

Sir Adam's old friend George Dempster of Dunnichen, formerly
M.P. for the Perth burghs and brother-in-law of Charles Fergusson's daughter Jean, sent his facetious compliments:

'I pray my sincerest congratulations to Lord Hermand. Bid
him think twice before he exchanges a pleasant walk on the
banks of Hermand for slaving away the heart of his spring and
autumn on the bench hanging, quartering and drawing traitors
and malefactors.'[1]

The period when George Fergusson took his seat in the
Court of Session was the last days 'of the undivided fifteen-
judge court, of written pleadings and of endless petitions',
whose disappearance Lord Corehouse, who retired from the
bench in 1839, remembered and so greatly regretted;[2] 'of a
mob of fifteen judges, meeting without previous consultation,
and each impatient for independent eminence,'[3] under the sage
and moderating presidency of Ilay Campbell, the best lawyer
of his time. The old Parliament House was still unaltered in its
exterior, and 'the haill fifteen' still met in the low, dark, square
'Inner House' which Cockburn describes as 'so cased in venerable dirt that it was impossible to say whether it had ever been
painted'. The atmosphere of the Court was one in which time
seemed to have stood still. This was the setting in which Stair
and Erskine, Forbes and Kames, had shone; it had scarcely
changed since Hermand's father Kilkerran had passed from it
forty years before. 'Very little fancy was necessary to make
one see the ancient legal sages hirpling through its dim litigious
light.'[4]

To enter on his career as a judge in a scene so rich in tradition
must have nourished Hermand's taste for the old ways and
unchanged methods of Scots law. It was not long moreover
before he began to add his contribution to the eccentricities
which flourished among the occupants of the bench, although,
as in his own case, not to the exclusion of professional ability,
industry, and integrity. Judicial eccentricity was perhaps rarer

---

[1] *Letters of George Dempster to Sir Adam Fergusson*, p. 274.

[2] Cockburn's *Journal*, vol. i, pp. 221–2.

[3] Cockburn's *Memorials*, p. 129.   [4] *Ibid.*, pp. 110, 111.

than it had been. The broad accents and homely humour of Auchinleck, Kames and Braxfield were stilled; no judge now addressed his colleagues, as Kames had done, by the affectionate epithet of 'bitches'; none now sat morosely at the clerks' table, as Monboddo had insisted on doing and thereby stirred his brother-judge Auchinleck to jests on the theme of '*De profundis exclamavi*'; and the judges had given up the practice of eating biscuits and drinking port on the bench during an unduly protracted cause.

Yet the bench which saw the opening of the nineteenth century had its queer characters: the Justice Clerk Eskgrove, with his long-winded 'charges', his mumbling speech, and his trick of superfluous epithets—'ane excellent, and worthy, and amiabill, and agreeabill, and very good man'; Cullen, whom Professor Dugald Stewart called 'the most perfect of all mimics'; and Allan Maconochie, Lord Meadowbank, who had a passion for wrapping up his arguments in metaphysical phraseology, and 'had more pleasure in inventing ingenious reasons for being wrong, than in being quietly right'. Young Henry Cockburn saw them all and committed them to his memory; and in his brilliant pages they live, move and speak again.

Hermand, a blunt and straightforward speaker himself,[1] had a violent dislike to 'that creature Meadowbank', and took every opportunity of pouring contempt upon his opinions. He once even went so far as to disdain the authority of an Act of Parliament because it was Meadowbank who had cited it. 'A statute!' he exclaimed. 'What's a statute? Words. Mere words! And am *I* to be tied down by words? No, my Laards'—so Cockburn renders his peculiar pronunciation of 'Lords'—'I go by the law of right reason!'[2] He had other means also of baiting his colleage, interrupting him, for instance, with such remarks as 'Your Lordship should address yourself to the Chair'; and in any dispute between them Hermand, according

[1] See the imitation of his style in Lord Corehouse's famous parody, 'The Diamond Beetle Case,' printed in *Kay's Edinburgh Portraits*, vol. ii, pp. 385–6, and elsewhere.

[2] Cockburn's *Memorials*, p. 137.

to James Maidment, 'was uniformly the aggressor.' Maidment gives in detail one instance of Hermand's badgering of Meadowbank:

' "Macer," quoth Meadowbank, in the course of his speech one day,—"Open that window." A few minutes had barely elapsed, when, taking advantage of a pause, Hermand roared out, "Macer, shut that window." Then came an order to open, —then to shut, and so on, to the infinite amusement of the Bar, but horror of the Bench.'[1]

The strangest instance of Hermand's behaviour on the bench is perhaps the celebrated incident recorded by Lockhart which probably took place about the beginning of 1813, when *Guy Mannering*, its authorship still unsuspected by the world, was in the first flush of its success. Hermand was one of its most fervent admirers.

'He could talk of nothing else but Pleydell, Dandie, and the high-jinks, for many weeks. He usually carried one volume of the book about with him; and one morning, on the Bench, his love for it so completely got the better of him, that he lugged in the subject, head and shoulders, into the midst of a speech about some most dry point of law; nay, getting warmer every moment he spoke of it, he at last fairly plucked the volume from his pocket and, in spite of the remonstrances of all his brethren, insisted upon reading aloud the whole passage for their edification. He went through the task with his wonted vivacity, gave great effect to every speech, and most appropriate expression to every joke.'[2]

No one can have enjoyed this scene more than the author of the book himself, who sat close beneath the judges at the clerks' table.

Hermand's appearance is described by Cockburn—'tall and thin, with grey lively eyes, and a long face strongly expressive of whatever emotion he was under,' a long neck, and 'thin and powdered grey hair, flowing down into a long thin gentleman-

[1] *The Court of Session Garland*, ed. James Maidment, 1871, p. 103, note.
[2] *Peter's Letters to his Kinsfolk,*, 1819, vol. ii, pp. 121–2.

like pigtail'.[1] The only portrait of him in existence, painted by
Andrew Geddes and preserved at Cumstoun in Galloway,
shows him as an old man, with a rubicund face, thin white
hair, and a somewhat frail appearance, suggesting that it was
painted in the last years of his life.

Kay's two caricatures of Lord Hermand, both of his right
profile, give emphasis to his long nose, thin but not sharp, and
impart to his mouth a pursed look as though the judge is just
waiting his time to deliver some devastating retort to whoever
is addressing the court at the moment.

Once Hermand had taken his seat on the bench, his passion
for farming was able to have free vent. He might thereafter be
seen regularly in his fields at Hermand during the Session vacations, wearing rough country clothes with a grey felt hat, and
carrying a hoe or a bill-hook; accompanied perhaps by his
famous church-going Newfoundland dog Dolphin. There was
no beauty in the fields of Hermand. Miss Fullerton, the
daughter of Lord Fullerton, who lived to be 95, recalled how
Dr John Brown, the author of *Rab and His Friends*, remarked
after his first visit to the house that the estate 'was a place the
foot of man should have passed over and never rested upon'.[2]
But to its owner it was, as Lord Cockburn put it, a paradise,
and he never tired of his occupations there. Once he so lost
himself in the business of slashing down weeds on his way to
church at West Calder that the congregation was 'skailing' by
the time he reached his own gate. But what chiefly emphasised
his agricultural fervour was the way in which he began to
maintain the character of the farmer in his town clothes.

'On the streets of Edinburgh it would have puzzled a
stranger to decide whether the lawyer or farmer predomin-
ated in his appearance. His deep 'rig-and-fur' black-and-white-
striped woollen stockings, and stout shoes, at once denoted
that he had other avocations than those of the Parliament
House.'[3]

In 1805 his town residence was at No. 60 George Street, and

---

[1] *Memorials*, p. 131.   [2] Private information.
[3] *Kay's Edinburgh Portraits*, vol. i, p. 395.

LAST SITTING of the OLD COURT of SESSION 11 of JULY 1808

LAST SITTING OF THE OLD COURT OF SESSION, 11 JULY 1808

Lord Hermand first on left, in front; centre, Sir Ilay Campbell, Lord President;
on his left, Lord Dunsinnan; fourth from the right, Lord Meadowbank

Caricature by John Kay

from 1811 onwards at No. 124,[1] but this was only a lodging for week-days.

'On a Saturday, when the rules regarding costume—never very strict among Scotch advocates—were so far relaxed as to admit of riding dress being worn under the long robe, Lord Hermand would appear in Court booted and spurred, with a riding coat of splendid hue—pea-green, bright mazarine blue, or "drummer's yellow", according to the fashion then in vogue, but always with buckskin breeches and top-boots, ready to ride off to his country house.'[2]

Edinburgh in the years following the renewal of the war with Napoleon in 1803 was a very lively place, and though Hermand was too old to join in the great volunteer movement, when 'Edinburgh, like every other place, became a camp, and . . . the side arms and the uniform peeped from behind the gown at the bar, and even on the bench',[3] he must, with his relish for society and conversation, have revelled in the bustle and variety of life which distinguished the ancient city in her last period of brilliance.

With position, comfort, society, a home of his own, and a happy married life, there was only one thing more that George Fergusson could want; but that was denied him. This frustration is recorded in a diary of family events by his sister's step-daughter Christian Dalrymple, the heiress of Lord Hailes, who wrote in 1801 of 'the prospect of our beloved Mrs Fergusson of Hermand having a child in the month of May. These hopes were quashed; she miscarried, and my disappointment was equal to her own.'[4]

Hermand was not, however, a lonely house. George's nephew James, who after the death of his father Charles Fergusson in 1804 was regarded as the heir of Kilkerran, was a frequent visitor (like other nephews and nieces of George and Graham),

---

[1] Williamson's *Edinburgh Directory*.
[2] Lieutenant-Colonel Alexander Fergusson: *Life of the Honourable Henry Erskine*, 1882, pp. 190–1.
[3] Cockburn's *Memorials*, p. 187.
[4] *Private Annals of My Own Time*, privately printed, 1914, p. 14.

often with his second wife Henrietta. Lord Hermand took a great interest in his nephew's career—and assisted him with much sensible advice in his rather frequent financial difficulties. He even connived at concealing some of them from Sir Adam, whose gout-ridden retirement at Kilkerran had set him somewhat out of sympathy with the younger generation of the family.

Hermand's interest in the parliamentary representation of Ayrshire remained as intense as ever in spite of Sir Adam's retirement in 1796. It is true that in 1799, when a by-election appeared likely, he wrote:

'My keenness in politics is certainly abated, else I should feel more strongly than I do, that none of our family are in condition to avail themselves of an opening so favourable, as what may soon present itself.'

But the chances of various candidates and the possible uses of the Fergusson interest in Ayrshire still occupied a large share of his correspondence. The Eglinton interest was now an ally instead of a rival, and Hugh Montgomerie, who had been Earl of Eglinton since 1796, had frequent discussions when he was in Edinburgh with Lord Hermand, and when he was in Ayrshire with Sir Adam, on the various ways in which their influence (which when combined was extremely powerful) should be employed. Hermand was keen that nothing should mar the working of this alliance with Lord Eglinton, for whom he had a warm affection. 'I like people who have been *steady*, and am sure Colonel Montgomery has been so,' he writes on 11 April 1796; and again in February 1803, 'Lord E. not only adhered religiously to his engagements, but went beyond them'.

Hermand also wished that the Fergusson-Eglinton interest might be used to give his nephew James a start in politics, but to this Sir Adam was opposed, and Hermand did not press the suggestion. One of the most striking things in Hermand's political correspondence is his loyal submission to any wish of his brother as the head of the family. 'Let the event be what it may,' he writes in his letter of 11 April 1796, 'I do not think I could bring myself to go in a different line from you'; and ten years later he told Sir Hew Hamilton of Bargany, who was anxious to stand for the Ayrshire seat and had solicited his support,

'It would not be proper for me to come under any thing like an engagement, on the subject of a representative, where, though my native land, I have no property of consideration, till I had previously adjusted with my brother Sir Adam.'

This family solidarity is expressed even more strongly in a letter to Sir Adam of 19 November 1809, written 'to get at the truth of the report of a vacancy in Ayrshire':

'I have such a horror of a family dividing against itself, and so strong a sense of your undoubted right to direct the conduct of ours, that you need be under no apprehension of my giving the least encouragement to any application, or going farther than a simple reference to you, who I know will receive any suggestions of mine in the same kind manner you have always done, and particularly on occasion of last election.'

His political interests were not, of course, confined to occurrences in Ayrshire. He followed all that went on in Parliament, and was a profound admirer of his friend Henry Dundas and of William Pitt. There is a well-known story of his excitement on learning that the Ministry of All the Talents, whose only merit in his eyes was for its promotion to the bench of his crony Charles Hay as Lord Newton, had fallen. The news reached the Parliament House early in the day, and Hermand hurried out to spread the glad tidings in the New Town. As he strode down the Mound he exclaimed jubilantly at the top of his voice, 'They're all out, by the Lord! By the Lord, they're all out— every mother's son of them!' A startled woman who heard him jumped to the conclusion that his excitement referred to the beasts in a travelling menagerie near by. Rushing to the tall figure of Hermand, she flung her arms round him, shrieking out, 'Oh, save me, then, and my children!'[1]

---

[1] Fergusson's *Life of the Honourable Henry Erskine*, p. 468, note; *Kay's Edinburgh Portraits*, vol. i, p. 395, note. In the latter the woman's words are given as 'Good God! We shall then be all devoured!'

Only three years before his death, when he was nearly eighty-two years old, his interest in politics was unabated, as is shown by his last surviving letter to his nephew Sir James Fergusson:

'The Parliamentary business in which I was lately engaged, took so much more time than I expected, as to put it out of my power to reach Ayr in due time.'

Lord Melville's impeachment in 1806 did not shake his faith in the worth and wisdom of his old friend. He visited Melville in early October 1807, at his new house of Dunira, where his host was living in retirement after the excitement of his trial and acquittal, 'surrounded with the society of some sincere and attached friends,'[1] who, like Hermand, could appreciate his new hobby of planting and gardening. On 11 October Hermand wrote to Melville's son Robert Dundas:

'I have been delighted with Dunira, which I look upon as a prodigy to be created from a desert in 25 years; I was happy to find Lady Melville in perfect health, and though little given to despair of the Republic, shall never forget the kind communications your father made me upon the state of the nation which, with his counsels, whether in an ostensible situation or not, promises, if Ministry continue to attend to them, to be greater, I now believe, than ever it was before.'[2]

Lord Hermand's appointment as a Lord of Justiciary was made on 13 August 1808, on the retirement of Lord Dunsinnan.[3] It was an eventful year in the history of the Court of Session. President Campbell resigned, to be replaced by Robert Blair; the Court was divided into two, which made the despatch of judicial business much more quick and convenient; and permanent Lords Ordinary were appointed. The last sitting of the old Court, which Kay has commemorated in one of

[1] Lord Melville to Ann Strange, 17 Sept. 1807 (Cyril Matheson: *Life of Henry Dundas*, 1933, p. 312).

[2] National Library of Scotland MS 1074, f. 76.

[3] J. P. Wood, *loc. cit.* Brunton and Haig, in *Senators of the College of Justice*, 1832, p. 544, give the date of the appointment as 4 August, and the *Scots Magazine* for 1808 (vol. lxx, p. 637) as 16 August.

his best caricatures, showing Hermand's familiar profile in the left foreground, took place on 11 July, nine years to a day since Hermand first took his seat on the bench.

'It was a striking thing, to one who reflected, to see these fifteen judges rise that day, never to meet on the old footing again. . . . I could not have conceived that anything so ancient could have gone out so quietly. It was the natural death of dotage.'[1]

Such were the reflections of Cockburn, the Whig and reformer, who belonged spiritually more to the nineteenth than the eighteenth century. Hermand would not have agreed with his estimate of the old Court. He admtted that the changes introduced were for the better; but to him they were not the beginning of much-needed reform, but the finishing touches which rendered the machine of Scottish law finally perfect. This is exemplified by his comment, written to Sir Adam on 19 November 1809, on the abortive scheme of Lord Grenville to reform the Court during the life of the previous government:

'I have not the same dread of Lord Grenville's attempting, should he again come into power, which I do not believe he will, not from his own conviction, for he certainly knows nothing of the matter, but from the suggestion of interested partisans here or in England, to overturn the law of Scotland by idle innovations, now that it appears to the satisfaction of all mankind, that with the moderate improvement that has been made, every thing goes on with the exactness and precision of a clock, leaving nothing to regret but the delay in the House of Lords.'

Further interference with the works of the clock seemed to him both unnecessary and dangerous.

'His Lordship was hostile to any innovation upon the law and practice of Scotland, and took every opportunity of censuring everything that might in the slightest degree trench upon them.'

Such is Maidment's statement[2]—it requires some qualifica-

[1] Cockburn's *Memorials*, pp. 244–5.
[2] *Court of Session Garland*, p. 184.

tion. Hermand was not always opposed to reasonable revision of the law, and in some cases his opposition to change actually arose from a conviction that the proposed alterations were reactionary. For instance, when a committee of the Faculty of Advocates recommended, in 1782, the amendment of the Bankruptcy Act of 1772,[1] he wrote to Sir Adam as follows:

'The alteration is I believe exceedingly disagreeable to the mercantile interest of this country. . . . I confess the idea seems to me shocking, that we are again to be brought back to the barbarous situation in which our law formerly stood. . . . I am confident that mischief will be done by a total abolition of sequestrations, which I think were of infinite benefit in 1772 [the year of "Black Monday"]. I always looked upon it as a providential circumstance that the Act was passed at that time, and I am persuaded that such an Act may be framed as will prevent the inconveniencies that have arisen from the present one, while it will bring bankrupt estates into much better management than they will be if left to be tore in pieces by the diligence of creditors as they were before the Act 1772 was passed.'

This was written on 4 February, and another letter to Sir Adam of 21 March on the same subject shows that Hermand was far from reluctant to criticise an existing law:

'I can entertain no doubt that, wise as our forefathers may have been, it does not appear in their system of bankrupt law, which in place of being contrived for dispatch and expedition, seems in its nature to be calculated to last to eternity.'

To return, however, to the period of the alteration of the Court of Session, there is no doubt that after this time Lord Hermand was strongly opposed to further changes in it. In the National Library of Scotland there is a draft memorandum bearing his signature, and countersigned by Lord Balmuto with the note, 'I approve of what is here stated,' which seems to belong to the year 1809.[2] It is headed, 'Observations on Sketch of a Report concerning the Forms of Process in the

[1] 12 Geo. III, c. 72.
[2] National Library of Scotland MS 1567, f. 126.

Court of Session,' and contains this very characteristic passage, marked, however, for omission in the fair copy which was to be made of the document:

'With all possible respect for the honourable and learned author of the Sketch I think it my duty to state, that the conclusion does not seem to be justified by the premises, nay that it is such as would tend to bring disrespect upon the Court and to encourage dangerous innovation.

'The words are "Upon the whole we are clear that a better mode of preparing causes in the Court of Session may be adopted than is at present in use".

'If this means no more than what is applicable to every human institution, that it is possible in theory to invent a better form of process, the observation is not satisfactory, because it would not follow that forms venerable from usage and which have been found to answer the purposes of justice as well as those of any other country in the world, should be altered in the expectation that something else may possibly answer as well, or better.—What we have seen is certain, what we may expect is contingent.

'But I strongly suspect that a bad use might be made of such a declaration if sanctioned by the Commissioners as giving countenance to an idea held out in more places than one, as if the administration of justice in Scotland laboured under radical defects, requiring a complete alteration in all its essential parts.—This I know was not meant, but it becomes every man who regards the interest of the law, and the people of Scotland, to remonstrate against incautious expressions, particularly when they come from those most capable of judging, and most desirous of supporting the dignity of the Court.'

The introduction into Scotland of jury trial in civil causes was the object of Lord Hermand's particular hostility. This is illustrated by one of his letters to his nephew, Sir James Fergusson, of 1 November 1814, in a sarcastic anecdote concerning 'my friend Sir Alexander Gordon'.

'One of his Stewart officers had committed, or was supposed to have committed an offence deserving to be tried by a jury.

Jury trial is a trial by our *peers*. The peers of *Stewart* officers
are *Stewart* officers. But as there are but two Stewartrys in
Scotland, those of Kirkudbright and of Orkney and Zetland,
the knight was somewhat at a loss. He could neither hold his
trial at Kirkwall or Lerwick, and there was a great gulph that
made it difficult to transport Stewart officers from Ultima
Thule to his court. Not being able therefore to attain absolute
perfection, he compromised the matter, by borrowing 15 sheriff
officers from Dumfries and Wigton. Whether this mummery
ever went farther, history is silent. . . .

'To be serious, alterations upon the practice of the law of any
civilised country are serious things, productive of consequences
which no man can foresee. On the general expediency of trial
by jury I have great doubt except in such cases where ocular
inspection of the subject of controversy is needed for the ends
of justice. In that light I hold every question of boundaries,
and several others that might be mentioned, to be.'

Bound up with Hermand's objection to changes in Scottish
law was a profound conviction of its superiority to every other
legal system, and in particular to that of England. Writing to
his nephew on 10 October 1814 he says:

'I do not know a better system of police than they [the leading men of Ayrshire] have established to their hands, by Acts
of the Parliament of Scotland, which have been in some particulars amended by a series of British statutes'; and again:
'No fund is so well managed, as that of the poor in Scotland,
under the care of the minister and kirk session, and the less the
heritors interfere with them the better.'

His admiration of Scots law is, however, more directly illustrated by the report of a speech he made in the Justiciary
Court at Perth during the spring circuit of 1811:

'Lord Hermand next addressed the Sheriffs of the three
counties included in this circuit, expressing his conviction that
the criminal law of Scotland was in many respects superior to
that of England. Its superiority in point of dispatch, had been
evinced, he said, this day by the trial of a criminal whose guilt
had been incurred not quite six weeks before. He condemned

the practice of private prosecution which still exists in England, and the late attempt to abolish "informations *ex officio*", which is the only species of public prosecution in criminal matters known to English law.'[1]

IV

The first meeting of the reformed Court of Session took place on Thursday, 20 October 1808, when Robert Blair presented the King's letter appointing him Lord President in place of Sir Ilay Campbell. At this and at a later meeting on 11 November, the Lords considered the necessity of new regulations for conducting the proceedings before the two Courts. In dividing the judges, care was taken, for the sake of peace and harmony, to separate Lord Hermand from his *bête noire* Lord Meadowbank; the former was placed in the First Division under the President, and the latter in the Second under the presidency of the Justice-Clerk Hope.[2]

Before the reformed Court sat for the first time, Hermand had held his first courts as a circuit judge. He took the western circuit, with Lord Cullen, who had assumed the Justiciary gown in the same year that Hermand first put on the Session one. Cockburn was Advocate-Depute, and has left us a picture of Lord Hermand at Inveraray, to which the judges proceeded after leaving Stirling, which is one of his masterpieces of description, as well as one of his clearest testimonies that, with Hermand, drinking never interfered with business.

Hermand, as has been mentioned, was a staunch Tory and warm supporter of Henry Dundas, who was his friend and had gained him his appointment. Cullen 'disclaimed exclusive fealty to Henry Dundas',[3] and there was a lack of sympathy between him and Hermand, so that they had not met except officially for several years. On 11 September, however, in the inn at Invererary, where Lord Kilkerran and Baron Maule had warmed to each other half a century before, they met at supper.

[1] *Scots Magazine*, vol. lxxiii, pp. 395–6.
[2] *Ibid.*, vol. lxx, p. 873.   [3] Cockburn's *Memorials*, p. 146.

'They were cold to each other at first, but at last liquor soldered them, and by two in the morning (John Richardson, Bell, and I alone being present) they were embracing and vowing eternal friendship, and toasting each other's wives, and giving us young ones imitations of the old lawyers. I scarcely ever saw such a scene. But it was not unjudicial in those days. Cullen was in bed all next day, and never saw his own Circuit Court, but the immortal head of Hermand was clear and cool next morning at six, and after a few hours of business and a long sail, he returned to the charge at dinner with a picturesque and cordial exuberance of spirits which the concentrated kindness and gaiety of all Argyleshire could not have equalled.'

The 'long sail' was a fishing expedition on Loch Fyne, in which Cockburn, who does not say in what condition his own head was, accompanied Hermand.

'It was a bright, calm day, and we paddled about the whole forenoon. I rowed. His Lordship brought up some great fishes, but not without many a drive, and many a loud direction, and not a total absence of abuse, from the fisherman, who was all deference to my Lord so long as no fish was on the hook, but no sooner saw that one was in danger of being lost by his Lordship's awkwardness, than his whole respect was forgotten, and he bawled, and shook his fist, and directed and scolded most energetically, to the learned judge's vast entertainment.'[1]

It was perhaps as a circuit judge that Hermand reached his chief celebrity and popularity. The circuit journeys, too, suited his tastes. The circuit dinners appealed to his love of society and conviviality—though Cockburn certainly exaggerates in saying that 'with him the jollity of the Circuit was the only respectable thing about it';[2] and during his stately travels he could compare the cultivation of Aberdeenshire or the Borders with that of his beloved fields of Hermand, and the woods of Inveraray and Dunkeld with his brother's and father's plant-

---

[1] *Circuit Journeys*, pp. 87–8; *Journal*, vol. i, pp.267–8.
[2] *Circuit Journeys*, p. 73.

ings at Kilkerran. Perhaps, too, the pomp and dignity of the judges' slow progress to Inverness or Inveraray or Dumfries harmonised with his love of tradition and his profound respect for the College of Justice. He may have agreed with Boswell that 'the Lords of Justiciary should not contract their travelling equipage into that of a couple of private gentlemen on a jaunt of pleasure, but should remember that it is the train of a Court, composed of different members. Formerly every one of the judges had his led horse, his *sumpter*, in the procession. The disuse of that piece of pageantry, may be forgiven though not applauded.'[1]

The led or 'decked' horse had been abolished; so had the running footmen; so had the covered waggon for the baggage of the circuit; but the judges had each an allowance of £150 for their expenses, with an additional £50 when they travelled the long northern circuit.[2] This was partly to cover their travelling costs, and partly to enable them to maintain the dignity of the Court by a proper show of hospitality at the circuit towns to the magistrates, the local gentry, and the officers of the garrison where such existed. Occasionally a judge of a stingy nature, like Eskgrove, grudged expensive entertainments and attempted to make something for himself out of the circuit allowance. But Lord Hailes, for instance, 'took pleasure in seeing his servants and carriages appear to advantage';[3] and those who liked to dine well and jovially, such as Hermand, did not spare the public money granted to them for that very purpose. Besides the circuit dinner, for which the presiding judge stopped the business of the court when he thought convenient, there was the supper, with less formality and greater jollity, after the day's proceedings were over. It often took place after midnight: a heavy meal of salmon and roast beef, claret and port, with a flourish from the trumpeters when the royal health

---

[1] James Boswell: *A Letter to Robert Macqueen, Lord Braxfield, on his promotion to be one of the Judges of the High Court of Justiciary*, 1780, pp. 25–6.

[2] *Ibid.*, p. 22.

[3] *Scotland and Scotsmen in the Eighteenth Century*, vol. i, p. 414.

was drunk. The weaker vessels, such as Cockburn, found it a nuisance, but to Hermand the relaxation after a long day of judicial business, the talk, the hearty good-fellowship, and the reckless turning of night into day, were a never-failing delight. Sometimes his colleagues left him to revel alone. Cockburn 'once heard the servant of his serene colleague Pitmilly, who had a strong taste for decorum and law, and none whatever for laughter or liquor, tell the chambermaid at Perth to bring his master a large kettle of warm water. Hermand, who was passing to his dinner at midnight, said, "God bless me, sir, is he going to make a *whole kettle* of punch—and before supper too?" "No, no, my Lord, he's going to his bed, but he wants to bathe his feet first." "Feet, sir?" exclaimed Hermand, "what ails his feet? Tell him to put some rum among it, and to give it all to his stomach!" '[1]

At Aberdeen there was an evening party, known as 'the entertainment', given by the magistrates for the court, of which Cockburn notes, 'On the whole, it was the most civilised magisterial festival I have ever seen';[2] and at Dumfries, Ayr and Glasgow there were circuit balls.

Always, when the judges and the other officials proceeded to or from the court-house, there was 'the procession'. Cockburn says that its progress was often less impressive after dinner than before, but as a rule it must have been a majestic sight: the mace, the sheriff or sheriff-substitute, the magistrates of the town, the judges, bewigged and robed, the advocates, the clerks and other judicial officers, all on foot, with a guard of soldiers generally, and at night always with an escort of torchbearers, proceeding to the solemn notes of the two trumpeters with the 'G.R.' on the breast of their coats.[3] Cockburn loathed the procession and rejoiced at its discontinuance; but it undoubtedly impressed the populace with the majesty of the law —once at least to an unfortunate degree, when a poor wretch awaiting his trial in the Ayr jail cut his throat in despair 'as he

---

[1] *Circuit Journeys*, p. 73.   [2] *Ibid.*, p. 329.
[3] Cockburn's *Journal*, vol. i, pp. 172–3; Boswell's *Letter to Lord Braxfield*, pp. 26-7.

heard the brazen sound which announced the approach of Esk-grove'.[1]

Roads were being greatly improved at this period; but none the less the journeys took a long time. Perth was a day's travel from Edinburgh, and to reach Inverness took four. 'Dumfries and Ayr were both unattainable in one day; and Inveraray was out of the world.'[2] It was a wearisome business to reach Inverness, and perhaps tempers were sometimes short when the northern court was opened. During his last northern circuit Hermand, in spite of his usual respect for the Church, brusquely interrupted the customary prayer which began the business of the court. It was Dr Alexander Clark, minister of the third charge of Inverness, who was officiating, a 'worthy fanatic' who had been rebuked at the bar of the General Assembly in 1824.

'The reverend gentleman was standing, as usual, beside his Lordship on the Bench, praying away, loud and long, as if there had been nothing else to do but to hear him perform, when Hermand gave him a jog with his elbow, and whispered, with his ordinary birr: "We've a great deal of business, sir." '[3]

It was from the northern circuit, between Inverness and Aberdeen, that Lord Hermand was summoned in September 1813 to the death-bed of his brother Sir Adam Fergusson, who died after a long illness on the 24th.[4]

Inveraray, Glasgow and Stirling were the towns of the western circuit. At Glasgow there were excellent inns, but the court-house, although rebuilt in 1810, was singularly inconvenient:

'The judges sat (literally) on the top of a staircase, and separated from the street only by a folding door, their only room for robing or taking refreshment was a closely adjoining water-closet, there was not a single apartment of any kind for counsel, or anybody, except two, that were got for the occasion each Circuit, one for the jury to be enclosed in, and one of

---

[1] Cockburn's *Circuit Journeys*, p. 327.
[2] *Ibid.*, p. 321.   [3] *Ibid.*, pp. 41–2.
[4] *Scots Magazine* (1813), vol. lxxv, pp. 794, 879.

about 15 feet square, for as many of perhaps 1000 witnesses as could be squeezed into it without respect to age, sex, or station, and for all concerned, except judges, and witnesses, and prisoners, that is, for counsels, agents, jurymen, and mob coming and going, there was only *one door*, and it placed at the greatest attainable distance from the greatest number of people. This cursed door made the Court just a street. There was a constant stream of jostling comers in and goers out, whose noise, from tongue and from feet, the thumbscrew itself could not have checked.'[1]

Tongues and feet were not always the only disturbance. It was in this court that the solemnity of the proceedings was once broken when Hermand was on the bench by the sound of a musical box giving forth the tune of a popular jig, 'Jack's Alive'. Hermand was properly enraged. 'Macer!' he shouted, 'what in the name of God is that?' Unable to detect the offending musician, the officer could only reply, 'It's "Jack's Alive,"' my Lord.' 'Dead or alive,' exclaimed the judge, 'put him out this moment.' 'We canna grup him, my Lord,' replied the helpless macer. 'If he has the art of hell,' rejoined Hermand, 'let every man assist to arraign him before me, that I may commit him for this outrage and contempt.' During the resultant confusion, the disturber of the judicial peace quietly switched off the music, and since he could not be found the business of the court was at length resumed. Hermand's indignation had not yet cooled down when, a few minutes later, the impudent lilt of 'Jack's Alive' once more resumed its gay 'six-eight' rhythm. 'Is he there again?' roared Hermand. 'By all that's sacred, he shall not escape this time! Fence, bolt, bar the doors of the court; and at your peril let a man, living or dead, escape!' The whole court was now in an uproar, but the owner of the musical box could not be discovered. 'Jack's Alive' was not heard again, and when the business of the court proceeded without further interruption beyond the normal, Hermand began to think his ears must have deceived him, and speculated whether the cheerful strains might not have

[1] *Circuit Journeys*, pp. 209–10.

been 'a *deceptio auris*, absolute delusion, necromancy, phantas-magoria'.[1]

It was in the Glasgow court also that a more than usual clatter of feet one day caused Hermand to demand the reason of it. 'It's a man, my Lord,' replied the macer vaguely. 'What does he want?' asked the judge. 'He wants in, my Lord.' 'Keep him out,' said Hermand abruptly, and went on with the cause. But the would-be spectator forced his way into the court, and a few minutes later a renewed distrubance broke out in the neighbourhood of the single door. 'What's that noise there?' asked Hermand, and received the reply, 'It's the same man, my Lord.' 'What does he want now?' 'He wants out, my Lord.' Hermand's patience gave way. 'Then keep him in,' he thundered—'I say, keep him in!'[1]

In this pandemonium Hermand conducted, during the spring circuit of 1819, what was said to be the most laborious circuit court ever held in Scotland.

'In the course of it sentence was pronounced on 32 convicts, and the cases of 17 more were otherwise disposed of; but from the humanity of Mr Hope, the Crown counsel, in restricting the libels, no capital convictions took place. During the trials, upwards of 600 witnesses for the Crown were in attendance.'[2] The confusion and bustle in the court on those days must have baffled even Cockburn to describe.

The southern circuit, to Jedburgh, Dumfries and Ayr, was probably the one Hermand enjoyed the most. True, it appears to have been on this journey that he once remarked that 'he always detected a royal burgh by its stink',[3] but it had more attractive features than the other circuits. At Jedburgh was Walter Scott as Sheriff of Selkirkshire, to enliven the circuit dinners with his tales and jests.[4] At Dumfries was the regular

[1] *Kay's Edinburgh Portraits*, vol. i, p. 394.

[2] *Scots Magazine* (1819), new series, vol. iv, p. 467.

[3] Cockburn's *Circuit Journeys*, p. 98.

[4] 'I am here at the circuit,' wrote Scott from Jedburgh on 21 April 1822, 'where old Lord Hermand is tremendously grand. He is the last of our old wild original lawyers. His lady who attends for

circuit ball, which Hermand, who loved to see young people enjoying themselves, must always have relished; and near Kirkcudbright was Cumstoun, the home of his wife's niece and her husband Thomas Maitland, who was later to be a judge as Lord Dundrennan. Thence the route lay homewards through familiar and beautiful country to Ayr, which was a very gay and sociable place.[1] After the autumn circuit business at Ayr was over, he could ride the fifteen miles to Kilkerran, where the square panelled chamber, known to this day as 'Lord Hermand's room', was reserved for him; and after 1813, when his nephew Sir James succeeded to the property, there would be a houseful of children for him to play with—or rather converse with, for 'he always treated them seriously, exactly as if they were grown up'. During a game on Sir James's new bowling-green with his grand-nephew Robert Duncan Fergusson, when he was eighty years old and the boy ten, Hermand once remarked, 'No wonder that that little fellow and I are such friends—there are just seventy years between us.'[2]

Lord Hermand continued his judicial career till he was eighty-three, resigning from the Court of Session in 1826. The serene close of his energetic life is best described by Lord Cockburn:

'He lived about eighty-four years, with keen and undisguised feelings and opinions, without ever being alienated from a friend, or imagining a shabby action, devoted to rural occupations, keeping up his reading, and maintaining his interest in the world by cultivating the young. Instead of sighing over the departure of former days, and grumbling at change, he zealously patronised every new project, not political; and at last mellowed away, amidst a revering household, without having

the purpose cannot manage to keep him sober a-nights, and two rascals having been tried yesterday for robbing an ale-house, he argued it was an almost irrefragable proof of their guilt that they had remaind an hour in the house drinking *one* poor bottle of ale.'— *Letters of Sir Walter Scott*, ed. Grierson, 1932, vol. vii, p. 138.

[1] Cockburn's *Circuit Journeys*, p. 245, and Cockburn's *Journal*, vol. ii, p. 90.

[2] Cockburn's *Memorials*, p. 140.

ever known what a headache is, with no decay of his mental powers, and only a short and gentle physical feebleness.' [1]

Scott is not the only supporter of Hermand's claim to be regarded as the last of the old generation of Scottish judges; of those who spoke broad Scots with homely phraseology and pungent humour, who conceived that the majesty of the law could support itself without any affected dignity of their own, who combined a respect for tradition with a taste for Tory politics, studied literature, philosophy or agriculture in their spare time, and drank claret by the quart. If not the very last of these—for Balgray, Balmuto and Glenlee might all be considered his rivals for that position—he was the most typical specimen of them all.

His end was as calm as he could have wished. Nothing disturbed his peace of mind, his consciousness of a well-filled life and of a career of duty completely and industriously performed. His wife attempted, a few hours before he died on 9 August 1827, 'to administer some spiritual comfort' to him; but he wanted none. 'You need say nothing of that, my dear,' he told her; 'I've made my peace with God in my own way.'[2]

He might have said of his spiritual state what he once declared in the Court of Session, after President Campbell had delivered 'one of his deep and nice opinions, full of qualifications and doubts'—'Thank God, I never doubted!'[3] True to this mood, the book he asked to have read to him on his deathbed was no work of devotion, no volume of sermons, not even the Bible, but the latest publication of his admired Walter Scott, the *Life of Napoleon*. Growing weaker as the August day waned, he passed at midnight into his last sleep with the casual words, 'I am dying—farewell.'[4]

'The world', wrote Cockburn to his friend Jeffrey, 'does not seem to me to be the world without Hermand.'[5]

[1] *Ibid.*, pp. 133–4.
[2] *Letters of Lord Cockburn to Thomas Kennedy*, etc., 1874, p. 180.
[3] Cockburn's *Memorials*, p. 136.
[4] *Some Letters of Lord Cockburn*, ed. H. A. Cockburn, 1932, p. 22.
[5] *Ibid.*

V

Such record of Hermand's life as has survived throws practically no light on how his character developed. He scarcely seems a solid figure, susceptible of examination, before the time when he became a judge, and his extant letters were mostly written between his fiftieth and eightieth years. We are therefore almost bound to accept the entertaining though highly coloured portrait of him as an old man which Lord Cockburn presents, though other records and the important evidence of his own correspondence will be found to modify it in some respects.

It is essential to recognise that a character like Hermand's is one round which legends are bound to gather. There is no reason to suspect Cockburn or Maidment of having unduly embroidered their anecdotes of Hermand, still less of deliberate invention; but not all of them are first-hand, most were not written down until many years after his death, and some are scarcely credible. We have, for instance, Cockburn's testimony of Hermand that 'his air and manner were distinctly those of a well-born and well-bred gentleman', which would be in no way surprising even without the evidence of the Kilkerran family papers of the care and sympathy with which Lord Kilkerran and his wife brought up their children. But it is hard to believe of such a man that he could, as in one story Maidment tells, so far forget his manners or his dignity as to chase a careless servant out of the room and downstairs before the eyes of a party of guests, leaping over the chairs and other obstacles that came in his way![1]

Again, take one of the best known of Cockburn's stories of Hermand's sayings on the bench, and compare it with a thoroughly documented record of his opinion on a very similar case.

'Two young gentlemen, great friends, went together to the theatre in Glasgow, supped at the lodgings of one of them, and passed a whole summer night over their punch. In the morning a kindly wrangle broke out about their separating or not separating, when by some rashness, if not accident, one of them was stabbed, not violently, but in so vital a part that he

---

[1] *Kay's Edinburgh Portraits*, vol. i, p. 396.

died on the spot. The survivor was tried at Edinburgh, and was convicted of culpable homicide. It was one of the sad cases where the legal guilt is greater than the moral; and, very properly, he was sentenced to only a short imprisonment. Hermand, who felt that discredit had been brought on the cause of drinking, had no sympathy with the tenderness of his temperate brethren, and was vehement for transportation. "We are told that there was no malice, and that the prisoner must have been in liquor. In liquor! Why, he was drunk! And yet he murdered the very man who had been drinking with him! They had been carousing the whole night! and yet he stabbed him! after drinking a whole bottle of rum with him! Good God, my Laards, if he will do this when he's drunk, what will he not do when he's sober?" [1]

Now here is the report of Lord Hermand's opinion at the trial of Thomas Whyte, midshipman in the Royal Navy, for the murder of William Jones, seaman, on the pier of Leith on 15 June 1814. The trial took place on 13 July, and on the following day the jury delivered a verdict of culpable homicide by a plurality of voices. 'It appeared', as one witness said, 'that the pannel had got a glass, and Jones also appeared to have got liquor.' Whyte had ordered the seaman to go on board the ship's boat, an order which Jones delayed obeying, as he was 'lying on the pier, and singing along with the rest of the boat's crew, and striking his hat on the posts'. Whyte at length lost his temper, and drawing his dirk stabbed Jones several times. Evidence showed that the midshipman had no enmity towards Jones, that he 'had an excellent character, was sober and good-natured, and was rather liked by the men'. As for Jones, he 'behaved very badly when drunk, was insolent to his superiors, and had been punished for it. Some days before the accident happened, Whyte had saved him from punishment', Jones being drunk and Whyte running the risk of a reprimand himself by not reporting him.

After the verdict, the judges delivered their opinions at length. Lord Meadowbank, who spoke first, said 'he was very

[1] *Memorials*, pp. 139–40.

sorry for it, but it appeared to him impossible that a less punishment should be inflicted than transportation for fourteen years. Transportation for life might be said to be necessary; yet he considered it would be pitiable to deprive so fine a young man of a chance of once more returning to his native country'.

Now here is a contemporary summary of Lord Hermand's opinion:

'Lord Hermand concurred entirely with the opinion delivered. The present was a striking example of the effects of unruly passion, and that in a man who bore so excellent a character. He was much struck with the evidence of several of the witnesses as to the excellent character for humanity, sobriety, and even indulgence and forbearance towards the unfortunate individual who met with his death at his hands. He was sensible that the pannel had not been himself at the time; yet still that was no excuse, nor no palliation, in the eye of law, in the case of murder. Another defence set up, was disobedience of orders on the part of the deceased; but, unfortunately, in the situation in which the parties were at the time, there was no necessity for so violent an alternative as that resorted to. He believed there had been no serious intention, upon the part of the pannel, to commit murder; but still the use of so deadly a weapon, and the defenceless state of the deceased, incurs a responsibility of murder. Transportation for life had been condemned by political writers as wrong, in respect few instances had occurred of any person having been reclaimed, who had been condemned to that punishment, all hopes of returning to their native land having been cut off. He would therefore agree with their Lordships, that transportation for fourteen years was sufficient punishment in this case.'

The Juctice-Clerk (Boyle) and Lord Pitmilly agreeing, Whyte was sentenced to transportation beyond seas for fourteen years.[1]

[1] Full report in *Scots Magazine* (1814), vol. lxxvi, pp. 519–24, 596–601. See also 'The Intemperate Midshipman' in Mr. William Roughead's *Mainly Murder*, 1937. There is a drawing of Whyte at the bar in *Kay's Edinburgh Portraits*.

Could both these speeches have been delivered by the same man? It is some reflection on the candour of Lord Cockburn that he does not mention this case and Lord Hermand's part in it. It cannot have escaped his notice, since he himself was one of the two counsel who defended Whyte.

Hermand's powers of hard drinking aroused the disapproval of Cockburn, and in a more pronounced degree of Mr W. Forbes Gray, who collected the best-known anecdotes of Hermand in his book, *Some Old Scots Judges*. Cockburn says:

'He combined strong Tory principles with stronger Whig friendships, and a taste for Calvinism, under the creed of which he deemed himself extremely pious, with the indulgence of every social propensity.'[1]

Mr Gray goes further:

'Hermand accounted himself a man of religion. He attempted to reconcile the irreconcilable—piety and inordinate affection for the wine-cup—and, in his own eyes, he succeeded.'[2]

This judgment has neither logic nor conviction. Hermand's religion was a practical one, strongest in the most essential part of the Christian faith: he did unto all men, except perhaps Lord Meadowbank, as he would they should do unto him. The 'taste for Calvinism' he inherited from his mother, whose upbringing in the Edinburgh of George I's time had been extremely strict, and whose pathetic comment on the death of her eldest and favourite son was:

'It would be the highest stupidity not to be deeply humbled under the mighty hand of God, who by this awful dispensation tells me that I have heinously offended, since I have drawn such a stroke from the Father of mercies, who does not afflict willingly nor grieve the children of men.'[3]

But in Hermand's attitude towards his fellow-creatures there was nothing of either the hard or the hypocritical. He had the charity that never faileth. 'His affections were warm and steady; his honor of the highest and purest

[1] *Memorials*, p. 135.
[2] W. Forbes Gray: *Some Old Scots Judges*, 1914, pp. 200–1.
[3] *John Fergusson*, 1727–1750, p. 199.

order.'[1] In his correspondence with his nephew James and his step-niece Christian Dalrymple he appears as the kindest, the most approachable of advisers—'a most active and sincere friend' is the latter's description of him—and Cockburn's statement that he was never alienated from a friend, nor imagined a shabby action, shows with what fullness and sincerity his duty towards his neighbour was performed.

Cockburn had two causes of prejudice against the man he none the less loved. First, he himself had a moderate head for drinking and Hermand an unusually good one, a relationship which not uncommonly produces in the former case a sense of inferiority and disapproval. Cockburn wrote, moreover, in a sober age, the early years of Queen Victoria, and Hermand flourished in a period when, as Cockburn himself testifies, hard drinking was so ordinary a diversion as to be unremarkable. An apocryphal anecdote of the time when Hermand became a judge and Cockburn was still a young advocate tells how Pitt and Dundas, the Prime Minister and his chief lieutenant, entered the House of Commons together one evening in so 'blind' a state that when Pitt hazily remarked,

' I cannot see the Speaker, Hal, can you? '

Dundas replied,

' Not see the Speaker? Damme, I see two! '

The only thing really remarkable about Hermand's drinking was that, like Socrates, he could keep it up all night without injury to his ability to tackle the next morning's work. But he was no toper. He did not drink for intoxication but for conviviality. Wine 'inspired the excitement by which he was elevated, and the discursive jollity which he loved to promote. . . . The cordiality inspired by claret and punch was felt by him as so congenial to all right thinking, that he was confident that he could convert the Pope if he could only get him to sup with him.'[2] Supper, the 'Roman banquet', was the sphere where he shone most brightly.

Cockburn's second source of prejudice against Hermand was his politics. He was as extreme a Whig as Hermand was a

[1] Cockburn's *Memorials*, p. 132.   [2] *Ibid.*, p. 135.

Tory, and Hermand was, moreover, an intimate of the arch-enemy Dundas, and had shown hostility towards Cockburn's idol Henry Erskine when he was removed from his office of Dean of Faculty. All Whigs in Cockburn's pages are models not only of virtue but of ability, and as a natural corollary the intellectual gifts of Tories are frequently underestimated. Hermand was not a great or brilliant lawyer; but as advocate and judge he was undoubtedly above the average, and Cockburn unduly belittles him in implying that his heart was so much better than his head that 'had he depended on his understanding alone, or chiefly, he would have been wrecked every week . . . . Like many other counsel, not of the highest class, he owed his professional practice chiefly to the fervour of his zeal.'[1]

This is an over-statement. We have the word of the Duke of Portland that Dundas wished to make George Fergusson a judge as early as 1796, and that of Robert Dundas, Lord Advocate, that he and Henry Dundas spoke of him as the obvious candidate for promotion to the bench on every vacancy that occurred between 1796 and 1799[2]—only his own wish preventing his elevation. Dundas never promoted a man out of friendship alone, and was invariably careful to ensure that such men as he advanced were worthy of their new sphere and would do credit to his choice.

Extravagances Hermand undoubtedly committed, and from them his legend has grown. Cockburn touched the root of it when he wrote:

'What was it that made Hermand such an established wonder and delight? It seems to me to have been the supremacy in his composition of a single quality—intensity of temperament, which was so conspicuous that it prevented many people from perceiving anything else in him. He could not be indifferent. Repose, except in bed, where however he slept zealously, was unnatural and contemptible to him. It used to be said that if Hermand had made the heavens, he would have permitted no fixed stars. . . .

'His eagerness made him froth and sputter so much in his

[2] *Ibid.*, pp. 133, 135.   [3] See *ante*, p. 99.

argumentation that there is a story to the effect, that when he was once pleading in the House of Lords, the Duke of Gloucester, who was about fifty feet from the bar, and always attended when "Mr George Fergusson, the Scotch counsel", was to speak, rose and said with pretended gravity, "I shall be much obliged to the learned gentleman if he will be so good as to refrain from spitting in my face." The same animation followed him to the bench, where he moderated no view from prudence, and flinched from no result, and never saw any difficulty.'[1]

Humour he certainly possessed, though perhaps, in a rather different manner from Falstaff's, he was less witty in himself than the cause that wit was in other men. He is said, however, to have been an excellent *raconteur*, and it is regrettable that although he knew Boswell, the latter did not record his table-talk. Scott alludes to a Rabelaisian jest of Hermand's in mockery of Lord Meadowbank's ornamental waterfall.[2] One of his early speeches as an advocate shows how he could take advantage of a ridiculous argument on his opponent's side, and twist it dexterously so as to display its absurdity with evident enjoyment.[3] And there is humour in his reply when Sir John Scott, afterwards Lord Eldon, read him a speech prepared for delivery before the House of Lords and begged his opinion on it—'It is delightful—absolutely delightful! I could listen to it for ever! It is so beautifully written! And so beautifully read! But, Sir, it's the greatest nonsense! It may do very well for an English chancellor; but it would disgrace a clerk with us.'[4]

He was capable, also, not only of sudden explosions of temper, but of real anger. When, in 1777, Sir Adam was maintaining 'the coal cause' against the tenth Lord Cassillis, and Henry Dundas and Ilay Campbell, engaged as counsel on opposite sides, laid their heads together in an attempt to get the two litigious neighbours reconciled out of court, George

[1] *Memorials*, pp. 132, 136.
[2] *Letters of Sir Walter Scott*, vol. iv, pp. 539–40.
[3] See *ante*, pp. 92–3.
[4] Cockburn's *Memorials*, pp. 136–7.

Fergusson, who was acting as his brother's agent, was deeply hurt at not having been consulted in the matter. His resentment grew to indignation at the thought that what this implied was a suspicion on Dundas's part that he would have hindered the reconciliation and tried to stimulate the quarrel. 'Of all characters I abhor that of an incendiary,' he wrote to Sir Adam on 7 July 1777. 'I hope they mistake me as much in thinking me capable of acting such a part as they certainly do you in supposing that you would allow yourself to be misled by me were I disposed to make such an attempt.' A week later his wrath at what he considered the injustice Dundas had done him had increased to a cold fury.

'If he thinks I have expectations from him, he is mistaken, and much more so if he thinks I will submit to be used ill by any man, upon so despicable a footing. . . . I would not have done what he himself did . . . for his *head*, however much he may value it, and I could wish *his* private letters were produced as mine were.

'I do not intend, upon reflection, to speak to the Advocate [Dundas] upon the subject, till he chuses to speak to me, when I shall take the liberty of asking an explanation of his conduct. . . . I may be mistaken in his motives, but I chuse to have them explained. . . .

'There is one thing I cannot and will not bear, that is being treated with neglect, or even with *suspicion*, for I think that is what I have met with in this case.'

Two days later, however, he brought himself to open the subject to Dundas, whose unfailing charm soon smoothed over the misunderstanding and restored their friendship to its old footing. Fergusson wrote to his brother reporting the interview, and one passage in this letter of 15 July shows how fundamentally sensitive was the nature capable of taking such umbrage.

'It would vex me excessively to believe that the Advocate should suspect that I would be *bad* enough to oppose a compromise, or that I had any hand in either making or widening the breach. He assured me that he did not entertain any such suspicion, which no doubt I must hold to be so, though after all, I will own I do not yet understand what he could mean—though to say the truth he seemed surprised that I should even *wonder* at any thing that has passed. But, as John Paul [an Ayrshire acquaintance] says, "my feelings are part of me," and the part, I hope, which I shall keep longest, and which I cannot give up to any other person.'

The final sentence is profoundly self-revealing. It is in the same key as the remark which he is alleged by Cockburn to have made on the bench, striking his heart: 'My Laards, I *feel* my law—*here*, my Laards.' To this intensity of feeling were due such faults as Hermand had, but in it lay also the whole of his charm. No man was more honest, more genuine, or more wholehearted in his enjoyment of life. He inspired even more affection than he gave. His pleasures harmed nobody and nothing but the conventions of a changing age; and 'if sack and sugar be a fault, God help the wicked'!

INDEX

INDEX